SOLVE EMPLOYEE PROBLEMS BEFORE THEY START

Resolving Conflict in the Real World

Rita—

E P R on!

my friend —

[signature]

SOLVE EMPLOYEE PROBLEMS BEFORE THEY START

Resolving Conflict in the Real World

Scott Warrick, SHRM-SCP, JD, MLHR, CEQC

Society for Human Resource Management
Alexandria, Virginia www.shrm.org
Society for Human Resource Management, India
Mumbai, India www.shrmindia.org
Society for Human Resource Management, Middle East and Africa
Dubai, United Arab Emirates www.shrm.org/pages/mena.aspx

BETTER WORKPLACES
BETTER WORLD™

This publication is designed to provide accurate and authoritative information regarding the subject matter covered. It is sold with the understanding that neither the publisher nor the author is engaged in rendering legal or other professional service. If legal advice or other expert assistance is required, the services of a competent, licensed professional should be sought. The federal and state laws discussed in this book are subject to frequent revision and interpretation by amendments or judicial revisions that may significantly affect employer or employee rights and obligations. Readers are encouraged to seek legal counsel regarding specific policies and practices in their organizations.

This book is published by the Society for Human Resource Management (SHRM). The interpretations, conclusions, and recommendations in this book are those of the author and do not necessarily represent those of the publisher.

SHRM, the Society for Human Resource Management, creates better workplaces where employers and employees thrive together. As the voice of all things work, workers, and the workplace, SHRM is the foremost expert, convener, and thought leader on issues impacting today's evolving workplaces. With 300,000+ HR and business executive members in 165 countries, SHRM impacts the lives of more than 115 million workers and families globally. Learn more at SHRM.org and on Twitter @ SHRM.

Library of Congress Cataloging-in-Publication Data
Names: Warrick, Scott, author.
Title: Solve employee problems before they start : resolving conflict in the real world / by Scott Warrick, JD, MLHR, CEQC, SHRM-SCP.
Description: First edition. | Alexandria, VA : Society for Human Resource Management, [2019] | Includes bibliographical references and index.
Identifiers: LCCN 2019012954 (print) | LCCN 2019015561 (ebook) | ISBN 9781586446307 (pdf) | ISBN 9781586463120 (ePub) | ISBN 9781586446321 (Mobi) | ISBN 9781586446291 (pbk. : alk. paper)
Subjects: LCSH: Conflict management. | Personnel management.
Classification: LCC HD42 (ebook) | LCC HD42 .W37 2019 (print) | DDC 658.3/145--dc23

Printed in the United States of America   FIRST EDITION
PB Printing   10 9 8 7 6 5 4 3 2 1   SHRMStore SKU: 61.19509

Table of Contents

Foreword   vii

Introduction   ix

Chapter 1
Why Emotional Intelligence? 1

Chapter 2
Neurology of Emotional Intelligence 21

Chapter 3
The Godfather Effect 49

Chapter 4
What Are Verbal Jeet "Kill Strikes"? 91

Chapter 5
The Three Styles of Communication 97

Chapter 6
Kill Strike #1 = E̲PR: Empathic Listening 131

Chapter 7
Kill Strike #2 = EP̲R: Parroting 145

Chapter 8
Kill Strike #3 = EPR̲: "Rewards" 153

Chapter 9
The Verbal Jeet Coaching Process 163

Endnotes   189

Bibliography   193

Index   197

About the Author   205

Other SHRM Titles   207

Books Approved for SHRM Recertification Credits   209

Foreword

After so many years in the human resources field, you really yearn to discover new concepts or proven methodologies that are impactful and provide tangible returns on investment—or ones that just make a significant difference to your employees and leaders overall.

I initially met Scott in my quest to help leaders and employees call out poor behaviors and conflict without trust erosion. We met at an HR conference where Scott was very real about getting your hands dirty and resolving conflict in the right way. The truth of the matter is that all employees are really assets, and if we can find the common ground around so many complex and volatile situations, then we really can drive the pendulum shift needed to build beyond the task that current employees were hired for, which could have true cultural implications for every organization.

Scott takes a very different approach to emotional intelligence (EI) as the foundation to resolving conflicts before they start. We've all seen a lot of emotional intelligence presentations, but Scott teaches EI in a way that goes beyond the traditional warm-and-fuzzy trainings we typically attend. He introduces truly breakthrough concepts supported with neuroscience and made practical with methodologies (such as Verbal Jeet) that are thoughtful, simple, and produce results I have personally witnessed at the organizational and individual levels.

Seeing this in person was a game changer for me, and I have been an EI advocate ever since. Scott's elegant fusing of Verbal Jeet and brain science has guided me through a very successful career during some extremely difficult cultural transformations. I credit a large part of my success in my professional and personal life to a happenstance meeting with Scott and I'm confident the same can happen for you.

Thank you, Scott, for all your passion and expertise on such a fascinating and vital topic.

—Barbara Purdom, SHRM-SCP
Vice President of Employee Experience &
People Operations, GoDaddy

Introduction

I have been in human resources for almost 40 years now. I have also been a practicing employment and labor attorney for well over 20 of those years. If there is one thing I have learned from my decades in dealing with people and their issues, it is that really, really smart people often do really stupid things. That is a rule.

In fact, as I progressed in my career and met more and more people in positions of real power and influence, I started to craft my theory of de-evolution: As people move up in the world, they actually tend to get dumber! Time has done nothing but prove my theory correct.

For example, I once had a client, the president and owner of a very successful import business, who had sex with a prostitute in front of his family and all of his employees on his 80th birthday just to prove to everyone that he could still do it. I have seen a president and CEO of a large furniture manufacturer remove the skull-and-crossbones warning labels from containers of highly toxic chemicals so his employees would use them to remove stains from his upholstery. I have seen a CEO actually spank an employee. I once had a city councilman openly berate the employees of the city, and then tell them, "I can talk to you however I want, but you have to talk to me with respect." This city only had about 150 employees, but it also had three unions. I have had clients tell me bald-faced lies, only for me to catch them later. When I asked why they lied to me, they would often play dumb and say something like, "Oh! Was that important?"

Time and time again, I would encounter people of superior intellect try to get away with things that would make a bright 10-year-old child shudder. It always made me scratch my head.

Then, about 15 years ago, a friend of mine, Dr. Sheri Caldwell, explained it to me. I told her that I didn't understand how such highly educated and intelligent people could do so many stupid things and do them every day with such pride.

"Oh, it's easy," Sheri told me. "They're emotional children."

That was it. She was right, and the fact that they were highly educated and held powerful positions only made their emotional immaturity worse. In other words: they just got too big for their britches. As I studied this subject more, and as I learned more about the human brain and how it functioned, the sun, the moon, and the stars all opened up to me. I could hear angelic music telling me, "That's right, Scott. Your species has not evolved. You are all cavemen in pants."

Clearly, controlling your brain—or more specifically, controlling your ego and emotions—is the real skill that needs to be mastered in life. The secret to being happy and successful does not lie in raising your IQ or being more educated. It became clear to me that while your technical expertise and your advanced education might get you in the door, your emotional intelligence keeps you in the door and moves you up the ladder.

The real challenge for humans was simply learning to walk erect.

We all suffer from a lack of self-control because we are all just a short sneeze away from being knuckle-draggers. This explains why the world is in such a state. The Equal Employment Opportunity Commission is usually running about 50,000 cases behind, and our court system is overwhelmed with all kinds of people trying to find some sort of justice.[1] When we don't feel these forms of redress are working for us, we are no longer willing to engage in substantive conversations—we're ready to lash out at whomever we blame for the issue, whether that involve an all-out yelling match, a stapler sailing past your head, or a bullet flying through the air.

Why do so many situations turn so violent? Because we are human, and it is in our nature to go right into fight-or-flight mode. It is our survival nature, as you will see in this book. We are simply not wired to calmly address and resolve conflict.

I later discovered that we can actually quantify and measure one's level of immaturity, or emotional intelligence, using emotional quotient (EQ) tests. I honestly could not be nearly as effective as a coach if it weren't for these tests. It is one thing to sit down with someone and point out that they are acting like a child, but it is quite another to show them quantified data about their behavior based on their own responses. This additional degree of awareness often has the desired effect on the subject. It is not easy to look at a chart that proves you really are like a three-year-old.

After spending years trying to understand, teach, and measure emotional intelligence for both myself and my clients, the next logical step to me was to use our EI to develop what I believe is our most important skill in life: resolving conflict. For years, I have tried to teach supervisors, managers, and executives how to resolve their conflicts. Besides learning and practicing emotional intelligence, conflict resolution is the most important skill anyone can have. Even though there are several supervisory and leadership skills one must learn in order to supervise people, learning how to address and resolve conflict is far and away the most important and lasting skill one can have as a manager or supervisor.

Because my undergraduate degree is in organizational communication, and because I have taken several courses in mediation and conflict resolution, I felt I was very well qualified to teach these classes.

I was not.

First, you cannot resolve conflict if you cannot control yourself, which is the core of emotional intelligence. Second, and just as important, every program I went to, every book I read, and every class I taught was too complicated. Some of the most popular books on conflict resolution simply have too many points for the reader to remember in day-to-day life. Whenever you find yourself in a conflict situation, which is pretty much every day, you have a fight-or-flight response, causing your logical brain to shut down. The vast majority of people cannot remember the "Seven Steps of Conflict Resolution," or some other lengthy system; it is too much to remember when you are a supervisor on the front lines and you feel you are under attack. I soon realized that what we all really need is a simple and accessible system that anyone can remember and use when we find ourselves in a distressful conflict.

That is when I came up with "Verbal Jeet," which consists of only three moves: Empathic Listening, Parroting, and "Rewards," or "EPR." Verbal Jeet can only help you, however, if you are already emotionally intelligent and can control your ego and emotions in conflict situations, which makes you the bigger person.

I honed this system and taught it to clients and audiences over the next several years. It was so simple anyone could use it … even politicians, if they wanted to. Unfortunately, far too many people revert to their fight-or-flight response when they find themselves in a conflict. Of course, we all fall victim at one time or another to fight-or-flight, but to rely on our base caveman instincts as the way to regularly resolve conflicts will destroy most of our relationships in life.

I have taught this system to my audiences for several years and have had a lot of success in getting rank-and-file employees, supervisors, directors, and executives to successfully resolve the conflicts they have with each other and with the customers. These are life skills, so using them in your private life can also be a godsend.

It is important to note that one must possess emotional intelligence before using their Verbal Jeet Skills. You must be able to control your ego and emotions to use them effectively. Personally, I do not go through a single day without relying on my emotional intelligence and using Verbal Jeet. It helps me in my private life, beyond the realm of coaching and training programs.

So, I decided to write this book. We live in a world where it is the norm to attack each other when someone disagrees with us, or to have the people we work with lie to our face and stab us in the back as soon as we leave the room. Something has to change.

In the end, we all need to evolve into civilized human beings and adopt a simple and effective method of resolving conflict.

It is time to grow up.

CHAPTER 1

Why Emotional Intelligence?

THE WISDOM OF THE DALAI LAMA AND RED FORMAN

Whenever I look to someone for wisdom and guidance, I often think of His Holiness the 14th Dalai Lama, the spiritual leader of the Tibetan people. I then think of the great American philosopher and smartass father Red Forman from *That '70s Show*.

My favorite quote from the Dalai Lama is: "Bad action gives rise to misery."[2]

I then turn to Red.

In one episode, Red discovers that his son, Eric, has been cheating on his girlfriend, Donna. When Red presses Eric on why he cheated on Donna, Eric says, "Look, it's just that all these things always happen to me. It's like I have bad luck or something." To that, Red replies, "Son, bad things don't happen to you because you have bad luck; they happen to you because you're a dumbass."

Not a day goes by where I am not inspired by Red's sound advice.

For instance, I was thinking about the Dalai Lama and his American counterpart, Red Forman, while having my car washed on a beautiful summer day. I drove down to the local car wash, left my car with the attendant, and went inside to wait while it was being washed. While I was sitting there editing a new training program, a large older man came walking into the office. He was in his mid-60s, about 6'3" tall, had thick gray hair, and was really mad.

1

Apparently, he had just retired. As a reward to himself for making it all the way to retirement, he bought himself a brand-new Cadillac. It was a beautiful bright red with a cream-colored rag top. It was gorgeous. Earlier that day, however, he had apparently brought his brand-new Cadillac to the car wash and, somewhere in the process, his beautiful new car got scratched.

Now, at this point, you need to ask yourself a very important question: "Does he have a right to be angry?"

Absolutely! They scratched his new Cadillac, a prized and very expensive retirement present. He had every right to be upset and angry. But think about it for a minute: what does the man want to happen now? What does he want the car wash to do about his damaged car? Clearly, he wants the car wash to fix his Cadillac. *But remember:* "Bad action gives rise to misery," and "Son, bad things don't happen to you because you have bad luck; they happen to you because you're a dumbass."

So, let's see how the man went about getting what he wanted.

Because he was justifiably mad, he clearly felt that he had every right to act however he wanted. He stormed into the car wash and saw the skinny, minimum-wage-earning, red-headed clerk sitting on the other side of the checkout counter. The man instantly started yelling, screaming, and cussing at the little clerk, who was probably no more than 18 years old.

Now, considering the fact that the clerk behind the counter is human and has just been attacked by this massive older man, he naturally became very defensive. It was then his turn. I mean, getting paid minimum wage is just not enough to put up with all this, right?

The clerk instantly started yelling, screaming, and cussing right back at the guy. And, just so he could top the old man, the clerk threw in a few disparaging remarks about the man's mother. Well, with that little dose of gasoline thrown on the fire, the situation ratcheted itself up yet another notch. Now the man really went off into a blind rage. It was bad enough that the car wash scratched his car, but for this clerk to swear back at him was inexcusable.

"I mean, how dare you treat me the way I just treated you!" was basically what the man was saying to the clerk.

It was now this man's turn to up the ante even further. He escalated the situation by pounding his massive fist down onto the clerk's counter, knocking over the little air freshener display. With that, the clerk saw that the man was turning violent. So, he ratcheted up the confrontation one more notch: he called the police. Within a matter of minutes, the police were there. By then, of course, the angry man had put himself into a full-blown tizzy. In fact, he continued to slam his fist against the counter and wave his arms through the air as the police tried to question him.

I promise you, that is never a good idea when the police are trying to talk to you.

The police promptly arrested the older man and took him away.

Now, can't you just see this guy sitting in his jail cell about 30 minutes later, after the excess adrenaline had drained from his body and his heart rate had slowed back down, thinking: "What happened? It's such a nice day. I'm retired. I got up and went to the car wash, and now I am in jail. What happened?" This was clearly a bad situation made worse by an emotional hijacking.

- Did the man have a right to be upset and angry? Yes.
- Was it important for the car wash clerk to know that he was upset, angry, and wanted this situation corrected? Absolutely.
- Did he have a right to scream, cuss, and slam his fist onto the counter? No!

It was at this point that the angry man's emotional system took control over his body and bad things happened. Are emotions a good thing? Is anger a good thing? Absolutely, but can you keep your ego and emotions in balance with your logic while you are engaged and trying to resolve a conflict?

In 349 BC, Aristotle wrote in his book *Nicomachean Ethics*, "Anyone can get angry—that is easy…but to do this to the right person, to the right extent, at the right time, with the right motive, and in the right way, that is not for everyone, nor is it easy." This was true over 2,000 years ago and it is still true today.

The man at the car wash had every right to be angry, but was he angry:

- **With the right person?** No. What could the clerk do for him? Nothing. This was an issue for the owner or manager.
- **To the right degree?** No way! He went way over the top. It is fine to get angry, but he needed to remain in control. Going Neanderthal on someone you are mad at is never a good idea.
- **At the right time?** No! He should have been more aware of his rage and come back later. He was not self-aware and lost it, all to his detriment.
- **In the right way?** No! Yelling, cussing, and hitting the counter in such a violent manner is never a good idea.
- **For the right purpose?** Yes. His purpose was to get his car fixed, but I also suspect another purpose at work was to make the car wash employee pay emotionally for damaging his car and to show the car wash who was boss. This is clearly an uncontrolled ego and emotional problem.

Logically, the man knew all of this, but he was not acting logically. He had been emotionally hijacked. He had turned himself into a three-year-old child because of his rage. In the end, all the man managed to do was make everything worse for himself. His rage took his logic away and transformed him into a dumbass, as Red would say.

CUSTOMER SERVICE IS EMPLOYEE RELATIONS ... AND VICE VERSA

I often get calls from potential clients who are looking to train their people in customer service skills.

"I know you do that emotional intelligence stuff and that Verbal Jeet thing to deal with employee conflicts, but we are trying to train our customer service people. Do you have anything for customer service people?"

"Sure do," I respond. "I just change the title of emotional intelligence and Verbal Jeet into employee relations and customer service."

I instantly have a new program. Actually, it is so obvious that it evades most of us: employee relations is nothing more than customer service turned inward, and customer service is nothing more than employee relations turned outward. The skills you use to resolve issues with employees are the exact same skills you use to resolve issues with customers, and vice versa. Because most people miss this point, I often have to coach someone who has been bullying their employees or coworkers. I always ask the person, "Would you talk to a client like that?"

The answer I always get is, "Of course not."

"Why not?" I then ask.

The bully usually just smiles and says something like, "Because it is a customer. Our customers keep us in business."

"Then what makes you think you can talk to an employee like that? Employees make up the biggest part of your budget. Once you include employee wages, benefits, taxes, workers' compensation, mileage, cell phones, training, certifications, and anything else that goes into the hiring and retention of employees, few other things even come close. And more than that, who do you think does the actual work around here? Who do you think actually executes your strategic plans?" I ask.

The person thinks for a minute.

I always ask the person, "What do you think we would do to an employee who goes up to a $10,000 copier and kicks all the gears into pieces because it jammed?"

"We'd fire the person. That's an easy one," the person always responds.

"Then what makes you think we would ever let you do that to a $30,000-per-year employee, much less someone who is going to help us reach our goals? And by the way, copiers don't sue you … and they don't come back and shoot at you either," I will remind them.

I then explain that if they went to work for FedEx as a new customer service representative, they would be required to go through its in-house training program. They would learn how to use a system very similar to Verbal Jeet (EPR = Empathic Listening, Parroting, and "Rewards") in order to more effectively defuse difficult situations with customers. They would train these new employees in how to keep their cool and not panic (Emotional Intelligence), how important it is to let the customer "sound off" (Empathic Listening) and to understand where the customer is coming from … even when the customer is wrong.[3] Of course, these same skills are to be used with employees, not just with customers. If every organization's culture made it clear that employees are to be treated like customers, most of our conflicts would be resolved and not escalated. Therefore, it is important to remember that learning emotional intelligence, or how to better control your ego and emotions, and how to use the three "Kill Strikes" of Verbal Jeet (EPR = Empathic Listening, Parroting, and "Rewards") are life skills, not just work skills. Whenever you find yourself in a conflict, you need to gain control of yourself (EI) and use your Verbal Jeet.

It will change your life.

GETTING TO FIRST BASE

BUILDING A CHAMPIONSHIP TEAM

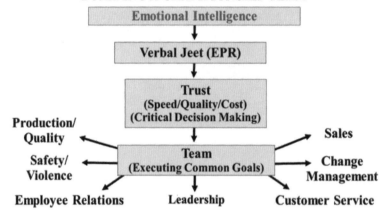

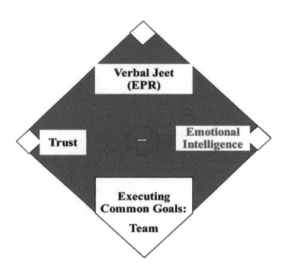

I have never met anyone who wakes up in the morning thinking, "I really want to screw up my life today. Things are going just a little too good for me right now, so I want to see if I can get fired, divorced, or maybe get arrested. That would be great." Still, millions of people do just that every day of their lives. They cannot control their egos and emotions, so they defy the wise advice of the Dalai Lama and Red Forman. In the end, they think they have bad luck or that the world is against them, but in reality, they did it to themselves. Likewise, every organization in existence has said that it wants to build a championship team. Amazingly, it will try to do that with emotional children and then wonder why nothing worked.

Whenever I see someone trying to reach their goals with emotional children, I always think of the movie *Butch Cassidy and the Sundance Kid*. In one scene, Butch and Sundance are hired to work as payroll security guards by Percy Garris. As they are all riding into town together to get the payroll, Butch and Sundance hang back, moving very slowly. Out of frustration, Garris turns and asks them what they think they're doing. Butch explains that they are trying to spot a potential ambush by Bolivian bandits. Garris is disgusted. He just stares at them and mutters his famous line: "Morons. I've got morons on my team."

Garris then explains that because they do not have any money going down the mountain, there is no chance of them getting robbed. No one is going to rob them if they don't have any money. They only have to worry once they have the money going back up the mountain.

Things will never end well for you if you are an emotional child or if you have emotional children on your team. You cannot be successful with morons on your team. Building a successful organization, or a championship team, begins with emotional intelligence. If you have emotional children or morons on your team, they either have to raise their level of EI or leave. It is that simple.

A great way to think of building a championship team is to think of baseball. In order to score, you have to get to first base, after all. In this case, getting to first base is becoming an emotionally intelligent person. Of course, getting to first base is easier said than done. Pete Rose, Major League Baseball's greatest "Hit King" of all time, accumulated an astonishing 4,256 career base hits and a .303 lifetime batting average.[4]

Think about that. The man who hit his way on base more than anyone else in professional baseball failed 70 percent of the time. Getting to first base and becoming an emotionally intelligent person by controlling our emotions and egos is the hardest thing most of us will ever do—and it is something none of us will ever perfect.

However, once you get to first base, you need to make it to second base, which means you now need to be able to resolve conflict by becoming a Verbal Jeet black belt. You don't want to be an "Attacker" (fight) and escalate the situation. One could think of Simon Cowell or the big guy at the car wash who thought it was a good idea to scream and yell at the little clerk, and later scream and yell his side of the story to the cops. These are the "I tell it like it is" people of the world, and it almost never ends well for them. On the other hand, you also don't want to be a passive-aggressive "Retreater" (flight) and suppress the conflict. Suppressing conflict only allows it to grow and eventually kill the relationship. Retreaters smile to your face, and then stab you in the back.

One of the most famous Retreaters of all time was Aunt Bee from *The Andy Griffith Show*. Yes, she smiled a lot and looked like a really nice old lady, but as soon as you turned your back, she would sit at the kitchen table with her friend, Clara, and stab you in the back.

Again, walking into a conflict and not running away takes emotional intelligence and self-control. You need to have the emotional intelligence to neither run away nor attack the other person if you want to be able to use your Verbal Jeet "Kill Strikes" to resolve the conflict.

This is no small feat.

However, once you have made it to first base, which means you can control your ego and emotions, you can now move onto second base, which means you can now use your Verbal Jeet "Kill Strikes" (EPR = Empathic Listening, Parroting, and "Rewards") to address and resolve conflict. Then, of course, you want to make it to third base and build trust with others.

What is "trust"? Trust means that the other person knows it is safe to disagree with you. You cannot tell someone to trust you. It must be built. It must be earned. You build trust with someone by proving to them that it is okay to disagree with you. Every conflict situation is really an opportunity to build trust, which means you are proving to the other person that you will not attack him or her for disagreeing with you, and you will not stab that person in the back later.

Proving that it is safe to disagree with you builds trust because the other person can reflect on their past experiences with you and know that it is okay to disagree with you, challenge your opinions, or come to you for help. It is safe.

That is what we mean when we say, "Trust must be earned." Real trust is built through conflict, not through agreement. No one believes anything you say. They watch what you do. In other words, the only time you build real trust with another person is when you are in conflict. We all can think of someone we have known for decades but feel like we don't know if we can really trust them. Why? Because we don't really know if it is safe to disagree with them.

Therefore, conflict is a vital part of building trusting relationships because it is the only time you have the opportunity to show that it is okay to disagree with you. This is how you make it to third base and build real trust with other people. Of course, you have to first be an emotionally intelligent person. You must then use your Verbal Jeet Skills and prove to the other person that it is safe to be honest with you and disagree with you.

And finally, because they don't give you any runs for just making it to third base, you now want to make it home. This is when you reach your ultimate goal: scoring. When you "make it home" and finally score, it means that everyone knows what the organization's strategic goals are and that everyone is working towards attaining those goals. Of course, the hardest part of this process is making it to first base (emotional intelligence) and then getting to second base (using your Verbal Jeet Skills). That is why this book will focus on getting to first base and then making it to second.

In short, the ability to control yourself and how you approach the person to address and resolve conflict is the most important life skill you will ever master … both professionally and personally. It will determine how happy you are in all of your relationships. In fact, it is so important in organizations that it is the number one skill managers must master.

In other words, if you cannot address and resolve conflict, you will never establish any real trusting relationships in your life, which is the very essence of happiness.

> *Likewise, if you cannot address and resolve conflict,*
> *you cannot be in management … period.*

HUMAN NEUROLOGY IS EMOTIONAL INTELLIGENCE

Becoming an emotionally intelligent person is not only the first step to building a real championship-level team, it is also the most critical. You cannot even think about building a team if you cannot make it to first base and surround yourself with emotionally intelligent people. If your team is filled with emotional children—people who cannot control their egos and emotions—it's game over.

Of course, since we humans are not wired to control our emotional system, becoming an emotionally intelligent person is the hardest thing most of us will ever do.

How important is your level of emotional intelligence?

At best, only about 20 to 25 percent of how successful you will be in this life can be attributed to your IQ. That leaves 80 percent that can be attributed to other factors.[5]

Clearly, most of these "other factors" are related to your level of emotional intelligence. In fact, according to Travis Bradberry and Jean Greaves in *The Emotional Intelligence Quick Book* researchers have discovered that 90 percent of the "high performers" in their database of over 500,000 respondents scored high in emotional intelligence.[6]

Years ago, Daniel Goleman, who popularized the concept of emotional intelligence, reviewed 181 competency models for determining job success. He then compared these 181 factors for job success across many different job classifications in all kinds of organizations. In the end, he found that 67 percent of these factors were actually factors of emotional intelligence. Goleman also mentioned another study in which 73 percent of the key abilities needed for job success were directly related to emotional intelligence.[7]

In another study conducted by Hay/McBer, hundreds of workers were subjected to in-depth interviews, extensive testing, and evaluations in order to determine the value of emotional intelligence competencies, as compared to factors relating to expertise and intellect. Overwhelmingly, the competencies relating to emotional intelligence were more than twice as important in reaching a standard of "excellence" than anything else.[8]

As far as the ability to be successful in any leadership position, it is clear that possessing the factors of emotional intelligence is more important than any other skill set. In fact, about 90 percent of a leader's level of success can be attributed to their level of emotional intelligence.[9]

Unfortunately, the lure of ego tends to overcome so many of us, which helps to explain why CEOs, on average, often score the lowest on emotional intelligence assessments. It is hard to have a great organization when it is being led by a child.[10]

Clearly, one's IQ takes a back seat to emotional intelligence in determining degree of successful job performance.[11]

On an even more important note, there has been a flood of research, including a series of studies conducted at Yale University, showing that emotional intelligence is not only important to your professional success, but it is just as critical to your level of personal achievement and happiness.[12] Of course, this makes sense. Whether it be your professional or personal life, you are dealing with people. That means it is important to build relationships and resolve conflicts.

CHRIS LANGAN VS. ROBERT OPPENHEIMER

In Malcolm Gladwell's book *Outliers: The Story of Success*, he studies the reasons why some people reach a high level of success and others do not. In one example, Gladwell compares the paths of two geniuses: Christopher Langan and Robert Oppenheimer. While Oppenheimer went on to become the "father of the atomic bomb" and famous throughout the world, very few people have ever heard of the smartest man in the world, Christopher Langan.

According to Gladwell, Langan was born a genius. By the time he was three years old, he had taught himself how to read. His ability to remember everything he read and heard and his ability to solve even the most complicated mathematical problems allowed him to breeze through school without ever having to take notes or prepare for any of his exams. Further, when Langan took his SAT exam, he received a perfect score.

Gladwell tells us that experts were stunned by Langan's mental capabilities. Naturally, they tried to measure his IQ. However, these same experts quickly saw that his IQ was so high that it could not be measured. In other words, Langan's IQ was off the charts. In an effort to attach some sort of measurement to his IQ, it was estimated to be somewhere between 195 and 210. This is the highest IQ score ever recorded, making Langan the smartest man to ever walk the planet.

Now, to keep this in perspective, Albert Einstein's IQ was about 150.

After finishing high school, Langan was offered two college scholarships: one to Reed College, a small liberal arts college in Oregon, and the other to the University of Chicago, a larger and more well-known university. Interestingly, Langan chose to attend Reed.

In his first semester at Reed, he got straight As. He had a perfect 4.0 GPA, which is what everyone expected from the smartest man anyone has ever met, Gladwell explains. However, towards the end of his second semester, Reed's administration told him that his mother failed to complete the required scholarship paperwork. As a result, Langan lost his scholarship to Reed. He did not take any of his finals his second semester and subsequently failed all his courses. He then dropped out of Reed.

Gladwell tells us that Langan returned to his home in Montana where he worked as a farmhand. He eventually saved enough money to attend Montana State University. However, after he started his first semester, his truck broke down. This made it very difficult for him to get to his morning classes. In order to help him out, a friend of Langan's agreed to give him a ride into campus every day. Langan's friend, however, could not get him to campus before 11:00 a.m. As a result, Langan missed all of his morning classes. Langan went to his advisor and tried to reschedule his morning classes for classes offered in the afternoon. The advisor refused to accommodate Langan, so, once again, he left school.

In the end, Christopher Langan, the smartest man to ever walk the Earth, never finished college. He never got the PhD he wanted. Instead, he worked as a bouncer for several years and now lives on a small horse farm in Missouri. However, Gladwell concludes that the reason Langan never reached his full potential had nothing to do with his IQ. Instead, it had to do with his level of emotional intelligence and his inability to solve problems with other people.

Unfortunately, many of his problems can be traced back to his childhood. Gladwell tells us that Langan's mother remarried several times as he was growing up. This meant he was forced to move frequently from one place to another, so he did not develop the interpersonal skills of building trusting relationships with others as a child. To make matters worse, Langan's stepfather physically beat Langan and his brothers when they were younger. In order to defend himself from his stepfather, Langan started lifting weights. Over the next several years, Langan put on a great deal of muscle. When Langan's stepfather started hitting him again, Langan punched him out cold. His stepfather left and never returned.

Now, can you imagine the worldview of someone who had to constantly defend himself in his own home? Your home is supposed to be your safe haven, not the place where you feel most at risk. Instead of learning how to effectively resolve conflict and keep his cool, Langan learned first how to retreat and then how to attack others to survive. He learned to use his brawn rather than his brain to resolve conflict. Langan's instinctual way of resolving conflicts (through his fight-or-flight response) was the death knell for his career, in spite of his tremendous IQ.

However, compare Chris Langan's childhood to that of physicist Robert Oppenheimer, another child genius who would go on to become the "father of the atomic bomb" and change the world forever. Unlike Langan, Gladwell tells us that Oppenheimer grew up in one of the wealthiest neighborhoods in Manhattan. His father was a very successful businessman and his mother was a successful painter. His parents sent Oppenheimer to the highly prestigious Ethical Culture Fieldston School on Central Park West. Oppenheimer's parents exposed him to a world where people persuaded and influenced others with their charm and intellect. He learned how to keep his cool and get what he wanted from others by using his powers of persuasion. Physical violence was not part of Oppenheimer's world.

Today, we call that "savvy," or emotional intelligence.

Later, when Oppenheimer was a student at the University of Cambridge in England, he tried to poison one of his teaching assistants because

Oppenheimer did not like a grade he received. As a general rule, when you try to kill someone, you get expelled, and you are most likely looking at serving some time in prison. Less likely is being allowed to stay enrolled at the scene of the attempted murder.

However, according to Gladwell, Oppenheimer avoided being expelled by convincing the school's administration that what he really needed was to attend psychological counseling. Amazingly, Cambridge agreed, saving Oppenheimer's academic career and his future while also changing the course of history.

Gladwell concluded that Langan, despite being the smartest man to ever walk the planet, never reached a high level of success because of his lack of savvy, or emotional intelligence, rendering him unable to resolve difficult conflict situations. Unfortunately, Langan didn't have anyone in his life who could teach him how to resolve conflict and control himself, unlike Oppenheimer. As a result, Langan, the smartest man you could ever meet, never graduated from college.

Think about it: Chris Langan was unable to convince his advisors to let him change his class schedule or resubmit his scholarship paperwork so he could continue his college education. Robert Oppenheimer, on the other hand, convinced Cambridge University officials not to expel him after he tried to kill a guy. The difference? Robert Oppenheimer could maintain his composure in a highly emotional and stressful situation and resolve his conflict with the university, thus saving his career. Langan could not.

THE GO-TO PEOPLE

Whenever I am speaking at a conference, whoever introduces me often mentions my law degree and my master's degree in labor and human resources. Interestingly, no one ever mentions my undergraduate degree in organizational communication. But as far as pure application goes, I use my BA in organizational communication more than the other two. Failing to remain in control of our egos and emotions is the root of most of our problems. In fact, whether we are successful and happy in life depends on whether we are able to master this skill.

If we can conduct ourselves like emotionally intelligent people, we have a much greater chance of building relationships with others and reaching our full potential. Unfortunately, most people often revert to their primary fight-or-flight response when they find themselves in a conflict situation, meaning they will either attack or retreat from the problem. That will rarely end well. People who can control their emotions stand out from the crowd. They tend to get what they want because they are much more persuasive than other people.

Therefore, even more important than our technical skills is our ability to remain in control of ourselves. If we can do that, we can build relationships with others. That is the first step in becoming a go-to person.

Several years ago, I met a professor (whom we will call "Dr. Groening") who had a very lucrative annual contract with a *Fortune* 500 consumer products company. His assignment was to spend two weeks at corporate headquarters every summer and analyze how communication moved throughout the organization. Each time, Dr. Groening arrived with a team of PhD and master's-degree interns to examine and document how communication flowed vertically and horizontally throughout the organization. They analyzed how employees communicated with each other and with their superiors, and how people in positions of authority communicated with their subordinates.

What I found to be most interesting from these studies was that Dr. Groening could accurately predict which employees were going to be either promoted or hired away into a better position with another company. Because he had conducted this study for several years, he was able to track his predictions and see how accurately he could spot upcoming and superior talent. In the end, Dr. Groening was right most of the time. He truly could identify the go-to people.

But how could this be? How could Dr. Groening predict who would be the up-and-coming and superior-talent people? How did he identify these go-to people?

When he and I discussed his work, Dr. Groening told me, "It's easy. It is not any great prediction. We were analyzing how communication in the organization flowed. So, we saw who everyone would go to for advice and assistance. Actually, all you really had to do was just watch each floor for a while. You would see whose office would get really busy. If an office consistently had a flock of people surrounding it, you just found your go-to person."

Dr. Groening told me that this person was always a good listener. This person could disagree with others while also protecting the other person's self-esteem, proving to everyone that it was safe to push back on their opinion or disagree with them. Of course, this person offered good advice to others, but more importantly, these people had savvy. They knew how to deliver a difficult message and make others feel motivated to improve. These go-to people gained everyone's trust. They stood out from the crowd because everyone could count on them. It was safe to go and see them.

Dr. Groening explained to me that sometimes this go-to person was a supervisor, but sometimes not. Actually, many times the go-to person was not the highest ranking or most senior person in the department at all. Regardless of the actual position this person held, two things were always true of these go-to people:

1. They were technically competent.
2. They were great interpersonal communicators.

Dr. Groening then made it clear to me that in most cases, the go-to person was often not the most technically competent person in the department either. Although this go-to person was always competent, others would not seek out the smartest technician if this person came across as egotistical, arrogant, or condescending. No one wants to get advice from someone who makes you feel stupid.

In other words, it did not matter how technically competent someone was if they did not know how to communicate with others in a way that protects the other person's self-esteem. All too often, people who are the most technically competent tend to only want to show off how much they know, or maybe use their knowledge to belittle others. This "Simon Cowell" attack style of communication could easily spell the end of their career growth—and it often did.

Go-to people are so highly respected that when they get promoted, almost everyone typically says, "Oh, yeah. I can see that." Go-to people stand head and shoulders above their peers due to their ability to communicate. As a result, few people are surprised when they get promoted. Almost everyone sees it coming, which makes them more supportive of the decision.

Dr. Groening also made another point very clear to me: go-to people get promoted first, even before their more competent peers and superiors because they build trust, so others go to them first. Unfortunately, go-to people are the exception, not the rule.

Years later, Dr. Groening's hypothesis would align with other research. In Daniel Goleman's *Harvard Business Review* article "What Makes a Leader?," Goleman reported that a study of 130 executives and managers found that the primary factor that determined whether others wanted to associate with them or come to them with issues was based on how well that executive or manager handled their emotions. If the executive or manager was an emotional child, others avoided them, regardless of their technical expertise. Whenever they needed help, however, everyone wanted to go to managers and executives who could communicate more effectively, not to some pompous blockhead.

In other words, Goleman concluded that they became go-to people. Dr. Groening also told me that being a go-to person is so rare that no organization ever has enough of them.

In the *Fortune* magazine article "Catch a Rising Star," Geoffrey Colvin took Dr. Groening's theory even further. In the piece, Colvin speaks with Tom Neff, a Spencer Stewart headhunter who specializes in recruiting the world's top CEOs. Neff says, "The style for running a company is different from what it used to be. Companies don't want dictators, kings, or emperors." Those days are gone. Companies don't want someone who just barks out orders. Today, companies want someone who engages with employees and asks probing questions. They want someone who will force the team to explore and find innovative answers to problems. Neff described this as being a more "subtle technique."

He then cited a survey conducted by Right Management Consultants, one of the largest outplacement firms in the country. This study showed that the number one skill companies are looking for in their managers is the "ability to motivate and engage others." Neff went on to explain that Right Management Consultants also found that 77 percent of companies say they don't have enough successors to their current senior managers who have these skills—just as Dr. Groening concluded years ago.

Today we see the same problem—there are still not enough go-to people to go around. In many instances, an organization has to turn to "second stringers" with inferior relationship and communication skills. Of course, the company Dr. Groening studied was a premier organization that valued the biggest part of its budget, which was its employees. So, it looks to these go-to people for leadership, unlike other organizations that tend to value only technical competence, like General Motors' traditional approach to management.

In the end, whose stock would you rather own?

Remember that at one time we thought, "What is good for General Motors is good for the country." No one is saying that anymore.

EMOTIONAL INTELLIGENCE AND PHYSICIANS

How important is it to become an emotionally intelligent communicator?

According to Malcolm Gladwell in his book *Blink: The Power of Thinking without Thinking*, the number one factor that determines whether a physician will be sued for medical malpractice has very little to do with their clinical skills. Instead, the most important factor in determining if a patient will sue a physician is how well the patient feels they are being treated on a personal level by their doctor. In other words, do patients feel like their doctor cares about them … or is the physician an arrogant schmo? Wendy Levinson is a medical researcher who, according to Gladwell, has recorded hundreds of conversations between physicians and their patients. She has researched numerous medical malpractice lawsuits and discovered an amazing difference between 1) highly skilled doctors who have been sued at least twice in their careers and 2) doctors who had committed many medical errors on their patients but had never been sued.

What was the real difference between these two groups of doctors? According to Gladwell, Levinson discovered that those surgeons who had never been sued spent approximately three minutes longer with each patient than those doctors who had been sued more than twice. The doctors who had never been sued were also more likely to make orienting comments to their patients, such as: "First I'll examine you, and then we will talk the problem over" or "I will leave time for your questions." They were also more likely to empathically listen to their patients. These doctors would say things like, "Go on, tell me more about that." They would really listen to what their patients were saying. These doctors were also far more likely to laugh and joke with their patients.

However, Levinson discovered that there was no difference in the quantity or quality of information they gave to their patients compared to doctors who had been sued at least twice. Patients don't file lawsuits against doctors because they have been harmed by malpractice. Instead, patients file lawsuits against their doctors because they feel they have been the victim of malpractice and they feel like their doctor simply does not care about them.

In *Blink*, Gladwell also turns to Alice Burkin, a leading medical malpractice lawyer, in order to determine why physicians really get sued. Burkin stated, "People just don't sue doctors they like. In all the years I've been in this business, I've never had a potential client walk in and say, 'I really like this doctor, and I feel terrible about doing it, but I want to sue him.' We've had people come in saying they want to sue some specialist, and we'll say, 'We don't think that doctor was negligent. We think it's your primary care doctor who was at fault.' And the client will say, 'I don't care what she did. I love her, and I'm not suing her.'"

That is the power of being an emotionally intelligent person and building relationships.

Personally, I have seen several physicians absolutely flush their careers because they acted like emotional children. On one occasion, I represented a hospital with a brilliant cardiologist on staff. We will call her "Betty." One day, a local farmer was scheduled to have a heart catheter put in place by Betty. While getting a heart catheter is not a huge procedure, this man and his family were unfamiliar with the procedure and had expressed anxiety about it beforehand. The farmer showed up at the hospital early on the morning of the procedure. His whole family was there to support him in his hour of need. However, Betty had gotten a call from her hairdresser that morning telling her that an appointment spot had just opened up that day. If Betty wanted it, she could have it.

Because Betty had been trying to see this hairdresser for weeks, Betty took the appointment. Betty contacted the farmer's family, who was already at the hospital waiting for their patriarch to go under the knife. She told them that she had to cancel the farmer's heart catheterization. Betty then told them that she got an appointment to see her hairdresser, but it would be fine because the procedure could be rescheduled. A little while after that, Betty went from making $800,000 per year to $350 a week on unemployment. Truly, the old adage of career success is true: You get hired based on your technical skills. However, you get promoted and are successful based on your ability to relate to others.

CHAPTER 2

Neurology of Emotional Intelligence

WHAT MAKES US TICK? THE NEUROLOGY OF EMOTIONS

BUILDING A CHAMPIONSHIP TEAM

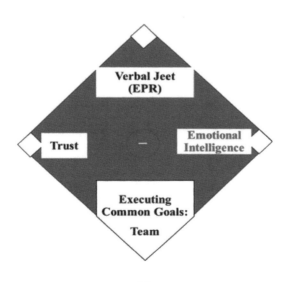

Whenever I teach a seminar on emotional intelligence, I ask the audience, "Which is stronger: our logic or our emotions?" Inevitably, the answer will always come back as a resounding "Emotions!" Clearly, humans are emotional beings, not logical ones. I will then typically ask the audience, "Well, did you ever wonder why that is?"

The audience ponders this for a minute. I then ask, "Have we evolved?"

I will then explain that I am not talking about Darwinism or evolution. Instead, I am talking about humans and how somewhere about 5,000 years ago, Fred Flintstone, a human, lived on this planet. If you believe in human evolution, then Satoshi Kanazawa's article "Why Human Evolution Pretty Much Stopped about 10,000 Years Ago" in *Psychology Today* is fairly important to you. Today, it is pretty much accepted among people who believe in evolution that humans have not evolved in at least 10,000 years. So, you also understand that the humans who lived here 5,000 years ago are like us today. However, if you are a creationist, then you don't believe that man has evolved at all.

So, everyone is in agreement: man has not evolved in the last 5,000 years. (It is important to note that when I use the term "evolution," I am referring to the DNA structure of a human being actually changing. We are bigger, faster, and stronger now than Fred Flintstone, but that is because of better living conditions, better nutrition, and so on. Since Fred's time, our DNA structure has not changed.) However, even though humans have not evolved in the last 5,000 years, the environment that we now live in certainly has—and not just a little. The civilizations we have built for ourselves in the twenty-first century are very different from Fred's.

I will then ask the audience, "So, when Fred left the hut every day, what were his biggest concerns?"

"Getting something to eat and not getting eaten!"

Yes! Humans were food!

The human brain of today still functions the same as it did back in Fred's time. Unfortunately, the same brain that served Fred so well by keeping him alive 5,000 years ago is not doing such a good job for us in the twenty-first century. When Fred Flintstone left his cave in the morning, he literally took his life into his hands. If Fred was going to survive the day and come home to see Wilma that evening, he had to rely on his highly developed primal ("primary," not "primate") instincts. We still exhibit the same primal instincts today that Fred exhibited, but we don't think about it. We just do them automatically.

To illustrate this point, I will often ask the audience if they have ever had "piloerection." There will then be a long pause. I will then hold up my forearm, feeling the hair on my arm and say, "No, it's not what you are thinking. Have you ever had goose bumps? 'Pilo' means hair," I will explain. "You don't command it to happen. It just does. It is an automatic emotional response." Other automatic emotional reactions we exhibit every day include these:

- When we taste or smell something bad, we purse our lips and scrunch our noses. We do this because when Fred tasted or sniffed something that smelled bad, the scent might indicate that the plant was poisonous, so his lips would purse and his nose would scrunch to keep the bad odor out of his nasal passages.[13]
- When we are surprised, our eyebrows immediately rise, our eyes widen, and we take in a deep gasp of air. Why? Because when Fred was surprised by a saber-toothed tiger, his eyebrows would immediately rise and his eyes would widen to let in more light, better illuminating his retinas and broadening his line of sight. He would also take a deep gasp of air to expand his lungs for fight-or-flight. [14] (That's probably what you were thinking, right?)

In Fred Flintstone's time, his emotional responses kept him alive. Why? Because Earth is covered with predators. However, compared to the other animals on this planet, humans are a joke. We can't run or jump worth a darn. We don't have claws. We couldn't climb a tree to literally save our lives. We don't have any fur to speak of, our teeth are pretty much worthless in a fight, and our vision and hearing stink. In short, humans are easy prey. Fred had a lot to worry about in just staying alive—but he did have some advantages.

First, God, Mother Nature, or whatever you believe in gave Fred a magnificent brain that was designed to keep him safe. Fred was given the largest set of frontal lobes on the planet. Our frontal lobes give us the ability to reason and figure things out—like how to build a house and a Smith & Wesson. (Believe me. If you are ever attacked by a bear, it is much better to have a Smith & Wesson than a stick. Just ask Leonardo DiCaprio's character in *The Revenant*.)

Just as important, Fred was also given an emotional system that was at least twice as fast as his logical brain.[15] Fred's brain was designed to react with emotions at an incredible speed and think logically later. Reactions that occur in 17,000ths of a second could keep him alive.[16]

In Fred's time, a hair-trigger temper could save his life. Reacting quickly and being wary of anything that was different from him, including other people, could have easily meant the difference between life and death. He did not have time to reason through his various options when he was being attacked by a saber-toothed tiger. He had to react quickly, and his brain was designed to do just that.

In other words: Fred didn't have time to stop and think. He needed to survive.

To illustrate this point, I will ask my seminar attendees if they have ever been outside in the summer and gotten bitten by a mosquito, just to turn and swat the mosquito before they even realized what was happening? That is Fred's emotional brain looking out for you. In short, all of these various primal reactions generated by Fred's brain were designed to keep him safe in a world full of tigers. Today, our brains react in the exact same way because we have not evolved at all from Fred's time. We are walking around in the twenty-first century with a brain that is thousands of years old.

Our society in the twenty-first century, however, is quite different from Fred's. We are no longer being chased by saber-toothed tigers. When we see someone who looks different from us, they are probably not trying to kill us, or eat us, for that matter. When we leave the house each day, the chances we will return home alive are much better than they were 5,000 years ago. The natural state of a human being is not to live in high-rise apartments, to drive around in cars going 70 mph, or to fly through the air. Still, humans are animals, just like all the other creatures that roam the planet. Today, however, we think ourselves "too civilized" to be compared to mere animals.

I mean, it's the twenty-first century. We are no longer wild animals—right?

The truth of the matter is that human beings are animals living with a 5,000-year-old brain. The natural state of a human is to live in a hut or a cave, make fires, hunt for or grow our own food, and fend off wild animals who view us from a very different perspective. Unfortunately, because we still have Fred's ancient brain structure, we also have his same primal reactions. The truth of the matter is that we have not evolved at all from Fred Flintstone's time.

R. Douglas Fields, PhD, an adjunct professor of neuroscience and cognitive sciences at the University of Maryland, College Park, and the author of several books about the human animal, believes that out of 1,024 other mammals studied on the planet, the human animal is seven times more homicidal than any other mammal. In his *Psychology Today* article, "Humans Are Genetically Predisposed to Kill Each Other," he states that humans are by far the most homicidal animals on the planet. This is because we have a 5,000-year-old brain that does not know it is living in the twenty-first century. It is our instinct to kill each other. Those same brain functions that served Fred so well 5,000 years ago are now working against us. Today, allowing these hair-trigger reactions to govern our behavior and giving in to our emotional impulses gets us fired, divorced, estranged from our children, thrown in jail, and worse.

That is one of the primary bases of emotional intelligence: impulse control.

However, there is one huge problem that we have to deal with when we try to conduct ourselves like emotionally intelligent people: we are human. That means we are hardwired to react emotionally to situations, not logically. In other words, we are working against human nature when we try to act like logical people. I will often refer to this section of the program as "Neurology for Everyone."

If you want to control your ego and emotions, it is absolutely critical that you understand how your brain works. Controlling your ego and emotions means you are really controlling your brain. This is what we call mental toughness, self-discipline, self-control, and many other terms. Humans are emotional people who think once in a while. We are not thinking people who feel. In short, we are just cavemen in pants … but it is time to evolve.

WHAT PARTS OF OUR BRAIN DO WHAT?

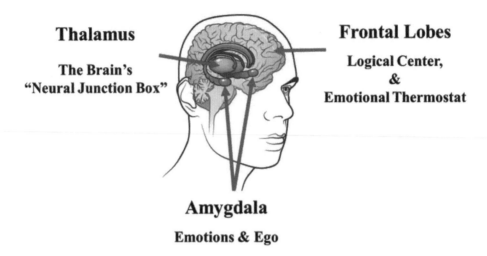

Thalamus

**The Brain's
"Neural Junction Box"**

Frontal Lobes

**Logical Center,
&
Emotional Thermostat**

Amygdala

Emotions & Ego

Keep this diagram in mind as we examine what parts of the brain do what.

WHAT DOES YOUR THALAMUS DO?

The thalamus, which rests in the center of the brain, plays a very important role: it is the brain's neural junction box. In order to understand human behavior and why we humans are as emotional as we are, it is critical that we understand how we are hardwired. Every impulse that enters the human brain goes to the thalamus first, where it is then hopefully redirected to the proper location. The thalamus is your neural junction box and works like the electrical box in your house. In your home, the main power source comes into the electrical box where the wires are then split and branched out to all the different receptacles and light switches throughout the house. Your home's electrical box acts like a large splitter, sending the various wires throughout your home.[17] That is also how your thalamus works. It is the splitter for your brain.

Therefore, the thalamus is in charge of directing the various stimuli that come into your brain and sending them out to where they need to go.

WHAT DOES YOUR AMYGDALA DO?

The amygdala's structure resembles two almonds resting on either side of the brain above our ears and behind our eyes and is part of the body's limbic system. Each part of the structure is about one inch in length, or about the size of a thumbnail. The amygdala acts as the link between the body's emotional system and the rest of the brain.[18] All of our emotions and ego originate in our amygdala. It is the body's emotional center. In other words, it reacts in response to pleasant and unpleasant sights, sounds, smells, tastes, and textures. Laughter, joy, anger, avoidance, ego, and defensiveness are all emotions that are activated by the amygdala. It therefore acts as the brain's emotional tripwire.[19]

The amygdala is also responsible for activating many of the nonverbal reactions we automatically and unconsciously exhibit, such as tightened lips and frowning when we are distressed, assuming a lowered defensive posture or crouching when we are attacked, wrinkling our nose when we smell something bad, pursing our lips and pulling away when we taste a lemon, and so on. These are all primal automatic reactions our emotional system uses as it tries to protect us from harm at 17,000ths of a second. [20]

It is also thanks to our amygdala that we can read the nonverbal cues of others, whether the other person wants to reveal them to us or not. Because our emotions are at least twice as fast as our logical brain, humans are simply not able to control our nonverbal microexpressions. A stimulus can enter our emotional system as quickly as 17,000ths of a second. Our frontal lobes can react, at best, at only half that speed.[21] Our expressions flash across our faces in microseconds, which is much faster than our frontal lobes can control them.[22] This is why professional poker players wear sunglasses in the Mirage Hotel in Las Vegas. (I don't think the sun shines too brightly in the Mirage or Caesars.) They realize how fast their microexpressions can rush across their faces, and they know they could not possibly control them consciously, so they simply hide their faces.

However, not only are all our emotions generated in the amygdala, but this portion of our brain also serves as one of the foundations for our social skills. For instance, studies with monkeys have shown that when their amygdala was damaged before the age of six months, those monkeys had difficulty adapting to social life. This is because the amygdala is necessary not only for experiencing emotions like fear, but also for recognizing the presence of these emotions in others and modeling their behavior. Problems in the amygdala have been associated with anxiety, autism, depression, narcolepsy, post-traumatic stress disorder, phobias, and schizophrenia.[23]

The size of an animal's amygdala also directly correlates to how aggressively and emotionally that animal will behave. Humans have the largest amygdala in the animal kingdom, which is why humans are the only animals on the planet who cry emotional tears. While other animals have tears and emotions, they do not cry emotionally.[24] For example, if you were to go home and poke your dog in the eye, yes, his eyes would tear up. But that is because you just poked your dog in the eye. Those are tears designed to protect his eyes. They are not emotional tears. (Of course, if the dog then bites you, we will see some real emotional tears.)

WHAT DO YOUR FRONTAL LOBES DO?

The frontal lobes control such functions as:

- Focusing our attention,
- Controlling our ego and emotions,
- Controlling our impulses, and
- Modifying our behavior.[25]

These are collectively referred to as executive functions. The frontal lobes in human beings make up 30 percent of the brain, which is the largest set of frontal lobes in the animal kingdom.[26] This is also why humans have such steep foreheads and why we can wear hats. You never see a dog or a cat wearing a hat that their owner hasn't attached to their heads in some way. Their frontal lobes simply aren't big enough.

At a fundamental level, how our brains work is so obvious that it evades us. Every thought we have is a chemical and electrical reaction firing in our brain. Basically, our brain is powered by glucose and requires an electrical charge to fire properly. It is also the hardest-working organ in the body. As a result, it burns about 25 percent of the calories you consume and 25 percent of all the oxygen you breathe.[27] In short, your brain is the true workhorse of your body. As a result, when you do not get enough water and nutrients, or when we have reduced blood flow in our bodies for any reason, the brain is one of the first organs to be harmed because it requires more resources than any other organ in the body.

Your brain operates much like a car, according to Professor Ryan Hamilton, a consumer psychologist at the Goizueta Business School at Emory University, in his lecture, "How You Decide: The Science of Human Decision Making." In order to operate effectively, your brain, and specifically your frontal lobes, works best when it has a full tank of resources, or neurotransmitters (what I will refer to as "gas"). If you run out of gas, your frontal lobes will shut down and your emotional system will take control. This is when really bad things happen. When we sleep, we restore these vital resources, transfer short-term memories into long-term memories, and give our brain the vital rest it needs in order to operate efficiently the next day. If you do not get enough sleep at night, you will not have enough blood flow to your frontal lobes the next day for them to work properly, which means you will not have enough oxygen to fully supply your brain as it tries to function. Good blood flow is critical for our frontal lobes to do their job.

Additionally, according to Dr. Daniel Amen in his book *Magnificent Mind at Any Age: Natural Ways to Unleash Your Brain's Maximum Potential*, when humans sleep, our brain clears out the excess cortisol that has built up throughout the stressful day. When you go into rapid eye movement (REM) sleep, which is the stage in which humans dream, your brain clears out the excess cortisol you have built up from the previous day.[28] When we do not get enough deep REM sleep, we feel grouchy because there is still too much cortisol remaining in our brain. Therefore, getting a good night's sleep is essential to becoming an emotionally intelligent person.[29] Sleep rejuvenates the brain. Without it, according to Dr. Amen, humans can actually become psychotic.[30]

In 1900, the average American got about nine hours of sleep each night. Unfortunately, by 2008, we averaged only about six hours of sleep each night. This lack of sleep greatly impairs our frontal lobes. As a result, we wake up in the morning with a tank that is already depleted.[31]

The left frontal lobe in particular has a very important job in relation to the amygdala. While the amygdala acts as the brain's emotional trigger, the left frontal lobe acts as the brain's neural thermostat for our emotions. One of the left frontal lobe's primary jobs is to keep our emotions in check, so it battles with the amygdala all the time. Humans typically experience about 150,000 emotions each year, or about 27 emotions every waking hour, all of which must be controlled by the frontal lobes.[32] That is one very important reason why you want to have a full tank and healthy blood flow and resources to your frontal lobes: to exert control over your ego and emotions. The left frontal lobe usually does a pretty good job of keeping the amygdala in check and is able to control all but the strongest of our emotions.[33] Think of it this way: what the amygdala generates, the left frontal lobe regulates. Unfortunately, it takes a tremendous amount of resources to keep our frontal lobes operating properly compared to our emotional system.[34] Our emotional system can pretty much run on automatic without consuming many resources at all.

The frontal lobes also work like a car's transmission. The more you change gears throughout the day, the more resources you will use. While it is true that focusing on the same project for hours at a time will greatly deplete the brain's resources, changing directions and dealing with many different issues throughout the day will deplete the brain's resources even faster.[35]

In other words, your brain works the same as if you were driving your car through the downtown area or on the expressway. If you are driving through the city, you would shift gears all the time, using up more gas. If you are going 70 mph on the highway, you won't burn nearly as much gas because you are not shifting your gears all the time.[36]

We make many kinds of decisions throughout the day. We control our basic urges to speak out and retaliate against others. We keep our mouths shut when we hear or see things that offend us. Unfortunately, by the end of the day, we have used up a lot of these vital resources. That is why it is so much easier to stick to diets in the morning than at night. This is also why it never ceases to amaze me that humans often save our most critical and highly emotional conversations until the end of the day when our tanks are almost empty. And then we wonder why these conversations don't go well!

Dealing with highly emotional situations also helps to explain why fights can get so personal and out-of-hand late at night. People are tired and have used up most of their brain's resources throughout the day, so the blood flow to the frontal lobes is greatly reduced. People get emotionally hijacked by their amygdala and end up repentant and embarrassed in the morning, explaining everything to the police … or a judge. Think of it this way: we all want to make sure our tanks are full when we engage in highly emotional situations.

In business, we often think it is best to deliver a written warning or terminate someone at the end of the day. This strategy can often end in disaster. The person who is facing discipline is tired and running low on glucose. Do we actually think they are going to process this highly emotional information in a logical manner? Whenever we are in a highly emotional situation, our frontal lobes, or more accurately, our left frontal lobe, has to perform double duty. We now want our left frontal lobe to catch a Hail Mary pass without enough energy to power it? That is just a bad idea all the way around.

That is one reason why we should never assume that because you said something, the other person processed that information accurately. *Remember:* humans typically experience about 27 emotions every hour we are awake, and all of these must be kept in check by the left frontal lobe. And now, at the end of the day, you want to deliver a highly emotional message to someone who is running low on gas? And you want this person to process this highly emotional information accurately and keep their emotions under control? And you don't want to get a coffee cup in the head or worse?

Good luck with that.

I prefer to handle highly emotional or difficult conversations at the beginning of the day when we are all fresh. If it is a written warning, I will then send the person home for the rest of the day to think about the problem. It is better to focus on the issue at hand in the comfort of your own home than at work.

According to the U. S. Occupational Safety and Health Administration (OSHA), our workplaces are already dangerous enough as American workplaces record over 38,000 physical assaults every week, and average about two homicides every workday.[37] These statistics alone are enough to make the case for having tense conversations early in the day on a full tank of gas.

We would never think of starting our car and traveling across town on an empty tank. (Well, most of us wouldn't. Some people, well …) Cars simply do not run when there isn't any gas in the tank. The same is true of our frontal lobes. To make matters worse for our logical brain, while humans need our frontal lobes to think, to reason, to exercise good judgment, and to make good decisions, we do not need our frontal lobes to live. Your body knows that. Your body knows that your frontal lobes are expendable as far as your survival is concerned. Therefore, when your body needs extra blood—such as when you have a fight-or-flight response—some of the first places from which your body takes extra blood are your frontal lobes and your stomach. This explains why we sometimes feel the need to vomit when we are nervous. There simply is not enough blood left in your stomach to digest your food.

When we feel we are under attack, we experience the same physical fight-or-flight response that Fred Flintstone did 5,000 years ago. Here is what happens:

FIGHT OR FLIGHT

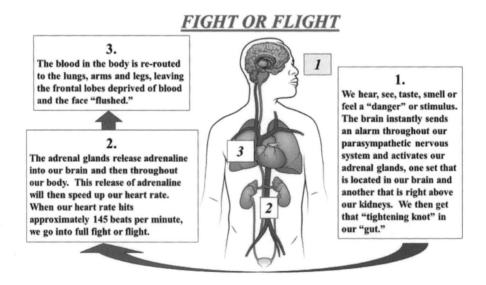

3.
The blood in the body is re-routed to the lungs, arms and legs, leaving the frontal lobes deprived of blood and the face "flushed."

2.
The adrenal glands release adrenaline into our brain and then throughout our body. This release of adrenaline will then speed up our heart rate. When our heart rate hits approximately 145 beats per minute, we go into full fight or flight.

1.
We hear, see, taste, smell or feel a "danger" or stimulus. The brain instantly sends an alarm throughout our parasympathetic nervous system and activates our adrenal glands, one set that is located in our brain and another that is right above our kidneys. We then get that "tightening knot" in our "gut."

- As illustrated in the preceding diagram, a stimulus enters the brain through either the skin, eyes, ears, nose, or mouth. Your brain senses a danger, so the fear response is initiated. Fear is the most primal and strongest emotion experienced by humans and initiates our fight-or-flight response.

- You have one set of adrenal glands located deep inside your brain that will release adrenaline or epinephrine directly into the amygdala. This is meant to engage our emotional system at an incredible speed, possibly as fast as 17,000ths of a second.[38]

- At the same time, because your body thinks it is under attack, your parasympathetic nervous system activates the adrenal medulla, which are located just above the kidneys.

- The adrenaline then circulates throughout the rest of the body. This is why you get that tight feeling in your gut when you get nervous, such as when you see a troll coming towards you, or on Sunday evening when you think about going back into that "pit of despair" on Monday morning. ("Troll" is my term for a bully or a problem person. Whenever you see them, your gut tightens up because you know what they are like and what they are going to try and do to you. Beware of the trolls!)

- This is your body having a fight-or-flight response. It senses danger and is trying to get you ready for battle. This adrenaline speeds up your heart rate and prompts the release of cortisol throughout your body, thickening your blood. (Now you also know why 20 percent more heart attacks occur on Monday morning than any other day of the week. Sunday night, sometime during *60 Minutes*, your gut tightens up over the thought of going into that pit tomorrow. Throughout the night, your blood continues to thicken until about two, three, or four o'clock in the morning then bam! You have your Monday morning heart attack. Of course, the bad news is that you just had a heart attack. The good news is that you don't have to go to work after all. Yes, as you get older, you really have to try and see the bright side of things.)

- Once enough epinephrine has been released into the body and your heart rate reaches about 145 beats per minute, your body will have a full fight-or-flight response. What does that mean? Your body's alarm system will be sounded and your amygdala will commandeer your brain. Your blood will be automatically rerouted to the large skeletal muscles in your legs, arms, and lungs, preparing your body either to go into battle or to retreat.[39]

- If this distress continues to increase and our heart rate hits approximately 175 beats per minute, most of us become what is called "temporarily autistic." According to Keith Payne, an assistant professor of psychology at the University of North Carolina at Chapel Hill, we become temporarily autistic in extremely stressful situations. We simply shut down and focus only on the immediate task at hand—blocking out all other external stimuli. Perspective abandons us, which can create a very dangerous situation.[40]

- This is when we feel like we are having an out-of-body experience. Everything slows down so we can give whatever is threatening us our undivided attention. Time seems to stand still. Everything becomes surreal. This reaction is designed to protect Fred when he is attacked by a saber-toothed tiger. Its purpose is to focus our attention on nothing else but the tiger.

- The adrenaline continues to build in our body and in our amygdala, until, voila! A fight-or-flight response.

Think about it. You just automatically rerouted the blood in your body to the large skeletal muscles in your arms, legs, and lungs, but your body did not make any more blood. So … where did the blood come from?

That's right: the brain! Your brain is impaired!

The blood just left your frontal lobes. Again, it is important to understand that your body does not need your frontal lobes to live. You need your frontal lobes to think, but as far as plain, old survival is concerned, they are expendable. So, when you have a fight-or-flight response, the body treats your brain, and more specifically your frontal lobes, like an extra reservoir of blood. If your frontal lobes lack blood, they will not function properly, meaning you lose much of your ability to reason and make good decisions. We then operate on automatic and reactive emotional functioning, which is why we revert to our primal instincts of fight-or-flight so quickly. This lack of blood in our frontal lobes is why we sometimes kick our cars when we get angry—we're nuts!

Again, how quickly can you jump into a state of fight-or-flight? Within 17,000ths of a second. Your heart can also speed up anywhere from 10 to 30 beats per minute. In other words, we can have a full fight-or-flight response and become emotionally hijacked almost instantly.[41]

Next, you will see two nuclear single photon emission computerized tomography (SPECT) blood-flow scans of the underside of my brain taken at the Amen Clinics in Reston, Virginia, to illustrate this effect on your frontal lobes.

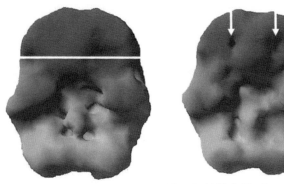

"Normal" Healthy Brain   **Brain With Reduced Blood Flow To The Frontal Lobes**

A brain SPECT scan is a sophisticated nuclear study that looks at cerebral blood flow and brain activity, or metabolism. These scans reveal the amount of blood flow we all have going to the various parts of our brain. As we know, blood flow to the brain is absolutely critical for one to think clearly and function as a human being. That is the problem with a stroke: a lack of blood flow to the brain. No part of your brain will work properly if it does not have sufficient blood flow.

It is largely because of nuclear SPECT scans and other types of modern brain scans that we have learned so much about how the human brain operates. We have actually learned more about how our brains work in the last decade or so than we have in the previous 5,000 years.

It is important to understand that a brain SPECT scan is quite different from computed tomography (CT) and magnetic resonance imaging (MRI) scans. CT scans and MRIs are basically anatomical or structural scans, which means they show us what is in the brain and what the patient's brain physically looks like. CT scans and MRIs will therefore reveal structural problems, such as concussions, clots, tumors, bleeds, and so on. SPECT brain scans, on the other hand, are functional scans. This means they show how the brain is actually functioning. In other words, you really can watch someone think. One important aspect of SPECT scans is that they reveal how well the blood flows throughout a person's brain. For the first time in the history of humankind, we can now look inside the brain and watch it work.

In these scans, my forehead is at the top and the base of my brain is at the bottom. This is as if you were lying down in bed with the back of your head resting on the pillow as you are looking up at the ceiling. Therefore, we are really looking up through the bottom of my chin into the underside of my brain. The scan on the left shows my brain at rest. Luckily, I have a normal and healthy brain. This is how a brain's blood flow should look. Notice how nice and full this scan appears. Don't pay any attention to the coloring. That doesn't mean anything. What you should notice is that I don't have any holes in my brain, which means that blood flow is nice and even. Again, if you do not have a nice, steady flow of blood into the brain, it will not work properly. The scan on the left also shows a white line running across the brain. This line marks the beginning of the frontal lobes. From the white line up, those are the frontal lobes, *and remember:* you don't need your frontal lobes to live. You need them to think!

However, the brain scan on the right shows a very different image. In this scan, you will see my brain after I have become really "ticked off." In order to "fire me up," the clinicians at the Amen Clinic gave me a computer game to play that I could not win, in order to make me angry and frustrated. That gave me a mild fight-or-flight response. As a result, much of the blood flow left my frontal lobes, the most expendable part of my brain, and went to my arms, legs, and lungs. This is what we experience, to one degree or another, when we have a fight-or-flight response.

Now, it is important to understand that these are not really holes in my frontal lobes, which are marked with the white arrows. When there is reduced blood flow to certain areas of the brain, the brain only appears as if it has holes in it. What has happened here is that the blood has been rerouted to my lungs and large skeletal muscles. As a result, the blood flow to my frontal lobes has been greatly diminished, and thus my ability to reason and make good decisions is greatly impaired. When this happens to us, our emotions overtake our logic. The amygdala can much more easily take control of our behavior because it can trigger our emotions long before the frontal lobes even know what is happening. In other words, when we lose our temper and go into a blind rage, we have been emotionally hijacked. All of this can happen to us within a fraction of a second because the amygdala can so easily overwhelm the frontal lobes and commandeer the brain.

In the scan to the right, I am, to some extent, temporarily nuts. In this state, people attack each other, kick their cars, punch walls, and so on. This happens to all of us at one time or another. This is the same reason why Michael Richards, the actor who portrayed Kramer on *Seinfeld*, had an emotional outburst while onstage and directed racial slurs against some black men sitting in the audience. During a performance on November 17, 2006, at the Laugh Factory in Hollywood, California, Richards's anger at being heckled by the men built, and built, and built, until his heart rate eventually hit (and probably surpassed) 145 beats per minute, sending his body into a fight-or-flight response. Blood in his body was automatically rerouted from his frontal lobes to his lungs and to the large skeletal muscles in his arms and legs. As a result, his neural thermostat turned off and his amygdala took over, which is, again, what we call an emotional hijacking.

In other words, there was nothing standing between his emotions and his mouth.

A similar process happens when you drink alcohol; because your body knows your frontal lobes are the most expendable part of your brain, they are the first to get soaked. Now you know why Mel Gibson went on his anti-Semitic rant against the arresting officer when he was pulled over for drunk driving on July 28, 2006. Because Gibson was drunk, there was nothing standing between his amygdala and his mouth. Thus, the real Mel came out.

This is why alcohol is really a type of truth serum. When the frontal lobes are soaking in alcohol, the real person comes out because the frontal lobes are no longer able to suppress their emotions. Nice, friendly people become nicer—they sing and are everybody's friend. However, angry people become mean. That is the real person coming out.

Therefore, when someone goes into full fight mode and starts verbally attacking others around them, it is absolutely ridiculous to think that this person will be able to process and fully understand what we are saying to them. Their heart rate is out of control, their body is undergoing a fight-or-flight response, and now the blood is draining from their frontal lobes, so they will not cognitively process what you are saying. Consequently, communication breaks down, tensions rise, the amygdala takes over, and bad things usually happen.

In other words, you cannot reason with a person who is "flooding."

It is also important to understand that we humans have only one emotional system. One. We don't have an emotional system for when someone physically attacks us and a different one for when someone verbally insults us. We have one fight-or-flight response. That is it. This is so obvious yet so easy to overlook. Because we only have one emotional system, our brain does not recognize the difference between someone punching us in the face and someone insulting us. Our fight-or-flight response is triggered in both instances. Consequently, every time you insult someone, demean them, or are intolerant of their opinions, you really are punching them in the gut.

This phenomenon is referred to as "endangerment." Our fight-or-flight response does not distinguish between a physical punch in the gut or a verbal insult thrown at us from across the room. Instead, it only reacts to danger. Whenever we feel endangered, our fight-or-flight response kicks into gear.[42] We don't think of verbal attacks in this manner, but we should, especially if you are trying to understand things like road rage and workplace violence.

THE SPEED OF THOUGHT

Now that you understand how blood flow and adrenaline works in your body when you have a fight-or-flight response, you should also understand why your emotions are so much faster than your logic.

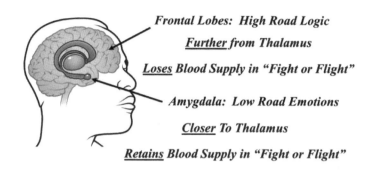

Frontal Lobes: High Road Logic
<u>Further</u> from Thalamus
<u>Loses</u> *Blood Supply in "Fight or Flight"*

Amygdala: Low Road Emotions
<u>Closer</u> To Thalamus
<u>Retains</u> *Blood Supply in "Fight or Flight"*

LOCATION, LOCATION, LOCATION…AND SPINDLE CELLS

One of the main reasons our emotional brain is so much faster than our logical brain is because of where they are physically located. As you can see by the diagram above, the amygdala is positioned very close to the brain's thalamus (or neural junction box) near the center of the brain. The frontal lobes, on the other hand, are positioned six blocks down the street. They are positioned about as far away from the thalamus as they can get.[43] As a result, an impulse can get into the amygdala in as fast as 17,000ths of a second from the thalamus, while it takes at least twice that long for the same impulse to reach the frontal lobes.[44] However, the location of these two neural systems is not the only reason for the lightning speed of our emotions.

Scientists have discovered an entirely new class of neuron called the spindle cell. Because the speed at which a neuron can transmit a signal to other cells increases with its length, the spindle cell's gargantuan dimensions ensure that it is faster than any other cell in the human body. Spindle cells are approximately four times faster than any other type of neuron because they are approximately four times longer.[45]

Think of the comparison between regular neurons and spindle cells like runners in a mile relay race in which the runners do not get tired, and all the runners are of equal speed. One runner racing one full mile will be able to easily out-distance four runners each racing for a quarter mile, and who must take time to hand off a baton three times. The team with the four individual runners will lose this race every time because the individual runners have to slow down to transfer the baton to one another. However, the single runner does not have to slow down to transfer the baton to anyone. That is how spindle cells work. Because spindle cells are longer than any other neurons, they are not slowed down by having to transfer its message as often as the shorter cells do.

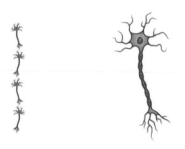

Common Brain Neuron   Spindle Cell

Thanks largely to these spindle cells, we can make virtually instantaneous decisions in 17,000ths of a second before our logical brain, or our frontal lobes, even knows what is happening. Neuroscientists now suspect that spindle cells are the secret behind the speed of our social intuition. They put the "snap" in our snap judgments because of their lightning speed.[46] Spindle cells are particularly thick and plentiful in the areas around the amygdala, which also helps to explain the speed at which our emotions surge.[47]

The chemicals transmitted by spindle cells only add to their central role in our ability to establish and maintain social connections. Spindle cells are rich in receptors for serotonin, dopamine, and vasopressin. These brain chemicals play key roles when it comes to bonding with others, falling in love, our good and bad moods, and our sense of pleasure.[48]

Spindle cells are crucial in making humans unique in the animal kingdom. Humans have about a thousand times more spindle cells than any other animal on the planet. Apes have only a few hundred. No other mammal on the planet has any spindle cells at all.[49] Consequently, neuroscientists tell us that spindle cells play a tremendous role in explaining why some people and primates are more socially aware and sensitive than others.[50]

If you look at the following diagrams, you will see the different paths our stimuli take when they travel the "High Road" and the "Low Road" in our brains.

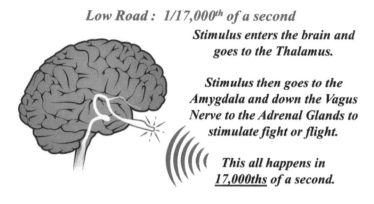

Low Road : 1/17,000th of a second

Stimulus enters the brain and goes to the Thalamus.

Stimulus then goes to the Amygdala and down the Vagus Nerve to the Adrenal Glands to stimulate fight or flight.

This all happens in <u>17,000ths</u> of a second.

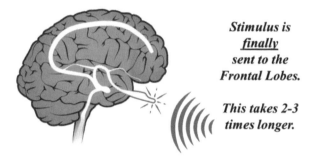

High Road : 2 to 3 Times Slower

Stimulus is <u>finally</u> sent to the Frontal Lobes.

This takes 2-3 times longer.

- Under ordinary circumstances, a stimulus of some kind enters the brain, either through the skin, eyes, ears, nose, or mouth.
- When we are not under the influence of a fight-or-flight response, the stimulus enters the brain's thalamus, which acts as the brain's neural junction box at the center of the brain. The thalamus then directs this stimulus to the frontal lobes for processing, where the stimulus is interpreted and sent back to the limbic system and amygdala. This route is referred to as the High Road, and it takes the stimulus at least twice as long to reach your frontal lobes as it takes this same stimulus to reach your emotional system.[51]
- Although the High Road to our frontal lobes is not very fast, it is very accurate because the frontal lobes (the brain's logical center) are being actively engaged.[52]

- However, when we are subjected to high levels of distress or perceive some stimulus to be a threat, our fight-or-flight response is initiated. As a result, an emergency, backdoor route is used to alert the brain of the imposing danger. When we undergo a fight-or-flight, or fear, response, the stimulus is still sent to the brain directly into the thalamus. However, rather than going to the frontal lobes first, the stimulus goes directly to the amygdala through a backdoor entrance. Because the amygdala is located very close to the thalamus, our emotional center can receive this message of impending danger in 17,000ths of a second by using the backdoor entrance. Our frontal lobes are at a huge disadvantage because they are located much farther away from the thalamus than our amygdala. It can take up to twice as long for this message of impending danger to reach the frontal lobes as it took for this same message to reach the amygdala through the backdoor entrance.[53]

Again, we have all experienced this phenomenon standing outside in the summer and getting bitten by a mosquito. When we get bit, we instinctively turn and swat the mosquito long before we cognitively know what is happening. This is Fred Flintstone's primal brain looking out for us. Our amygdala, or our emotional center, can react as quickly as 17,000ths of a second to protect us from harm, while our slower frontal lobes take at least twice as long to react.

This phenomenon is also why we get startled. We enter a darkened room, we see something that moves and instantly go on high alert. Our body tenses, our pulse races, our heart feels like it is going to jump out of our chest, and we gasp a deep breath of air only to discover that it was just the cat. Why were we afraid of the cat? Because Fred's emotional brain kicked in to save us before our logical frontal lobes could figure out that it was only a cat and not a saber-toothed tiger. It takes that long for our logical brain to catch up.

Another thing we now know about the amygdala is that it has a memory system of its own. It does not need the frontal lobes to function; this is due to our need for consistency and deep resistance to change.

Dr. Joseph LeDoux was the first scientist to discover the key role the amygdala plays in our emotional brain. In one experiment conducted by Dr. LeDoux, people were shown flash cards with certain geometric shapes. However, these people were shown the various shapes so quickly that they did not have any conscious memory of having seen them. When the subjects were shown these same geometric shapes later, however, they preferred the shapes that were flashed in front of them over the other shapes that they had not seen previously. Therefore, even though these people had no conscious memory of having seen these shapes, their amygdala's subconscious memory did see them and remembered them later. Because the human emotional system likes familiarity, the people gravitated towards the shapes their subconscious mind saw and remembered.[54] In other words, the subconscious mind is very real and exerts a tremendous influence over our behavior, whether we want to admit it or not.

Marketing professionals have understood this concept for years. Consider the beer industry. Everywhere you look, you will see commercials for beer. Commercials for Miller, Budweiser, Coors, and so on are all around us. Why? Don't think for a minute that these companies expect you to get up off your couch and run down to your local grocery store to buy their product when you see their commercial on TV. Instead, what they expect to happen is that you remember their ad or their slogan when you want to buy beer in the grocery store.

It is called branding, and Madison Avenue is very good at it. It works like this:

Everywhere you go, you see Budweiser, Budweiser, Budweiser. Then, the next time you are in the grocery store, you pass by the beer section and think, "Hey! I think I would like to get some Budweiser!" The next thing you know, you buy Budweiser. The trick in advertising is to get you to see Budweiser's logo more than anyone else so theirs will be the first one you identify when you are shopping. We have all fallen victim to this type of brainwashing. We can all remember certain advertising catch phrases:

- Nike: "Just Do It," or the "swoosh" logo
- Burger King: "Have It Your Way," or "Home of the Whopper"
- Alka Seltzer: "Plop, plop, fizz, fizz. Oh, what a relief it is!"
- Disney World: "Happiest Place on Earth"
- McDonald's: you just see Ronald

It's actually pretty easy to become branded or "programmed" because our amygdala is very susceptible to making quick emotional responses before our frontal lobes have had a chance to engage. This constant barrage of advertising rewires our amygdala so we feel an attachment to these products in our subconscious.

To demonstrate how effective branding, or "priming," is and to show how much faster the amygdala is than our frontal lobes, I will lead my audience in saying the word "pin" ten times quickly. I will then ask them a question to see how long it takes them to answer. You can try it as well by quickly saying "pin" several times in a row.

Now, what's an aluminum can made of?

Well…how did you do? An aluminum can is made of aluminum, not tin, right?

Of course, the vast majority of the attendees get it wrong, and they laugh. They know they have been tricked. Yes, our amygdala has a subconscious memory of its own that is much faster than our conscious brain, and it usually controls our behavior without us even knowing it. I then tell the audience that we will do another one, but this time they will get it right.

I tell the attendees that I am going to give them another word to say ten times and then ask a question, but no one is to answer for five seconds. Why? Because it takes about that long for the frontal lobes, our logical brain, to catch up with the amygdala, our emotional brain.

I then lead everyone in saying "top" ten times.

"What do you do you do at a green light?" I ask, before shouting "Nobody say anything! Think about it for five seconds!" Everyone then thinks for about five full seconds.

I will then calmly ask everyone again, "Okay. What do you do you do at a green light?"

They then say "Go."

I then ask the audience, "How many people really wanted to say 'stop'?"

This exercise works because of the amygdala. The amygdala can be programmed to respond automatically through our subconscious because it is a defense mechanism designed to protect us. We automatically react without using our logical brain.

Again, our amygdala can react at least twice as fast as our frontal lobes. So, when we simply react without stopping to think, our emotions are running the show. We are using the infamous Low Road. The Low Road, as you recall, is very fast, but not very accurate. Therefore, what we gain in speed by using our emotional system to react to situations, we lose in accuracy. In short, it is just another type of emotional hijacking.

When we stop and think for a minute, what we lose in speed, we gain in the accuracy of the frontal lobes, or the High Road. The ability to slow down and think allows your frontal lobes to take control of your emotional brain and many of the subconscious thoughts that live there. That is why the difference between success and failure, and the difference between being happy and being miserable is five seconds. Slowing down and thinking for just five seconds allows your frontal lobes to better control your emotional system—if your frontal lobes are operating with a full tank.

So, unless your life really is in danger, since we are all human, our first reaction to any conflict is always wrong! Think about it. Whenever someone disagrees with us, our gut tightens up, our blood pressure goes up and our palms start to sweat. Why? Because we are getting ready to attack and maybe kill the other person. That is why we need to take five seconds … stop … and let our frontal lobes catch up. That is why the difference between success and failure is five seconds.

However, most of us have been driving on the highway at about 70 mph when someone, someone who is usually on their cell phone, starts to come into our lane. With cat-like reflexes, in 17,000ths of a second, you were able to look into your rearview mirror, look into your side view mirror, and then swerve out of the way into safety. That is Fred Flintstone's brain looking out for you. You didn't have time to stop and think because your life really was in danger. You had to move … and your emotional brain took over. That is good.

However, in all other conflict situations, we need to stop and think for at least five seconds because our initial reaction is always wrong. That is the essence of emotional intelligence.

In order to keep all this in perspective, Dr. Daniel Amen tells us in his book *Change Your Brain, Change Your Life,* that our thoughts can travel as fast as 268 miles per hour—which is faster than race cars at the Indianapolis 500.[55] However, at best, humans can listen to about 400 words per minute.[56] Because our mind can race through several thoughts in just a split second, talking out loud is a much slower and more thoughtful process. We can only talk at about 125 words per minute. Therefore, coaching or talking to yourself will slow your thoughts down to the point where your frontal lobes can gain much better control of your emotions, organize them, reason through them, and control them.[57]

That is why you will often see some of the best self-help strategies for increasing your level of emotional intelligence are talking to yourself, using a sounding board, finding a mentor, or meditation, all of which force you to slow down and organize your thoughts. Better yet, when you take the time to write down what you are thinking and feeling, your brain slows down to a creeping crawl. Your hand cannot move anywhere close to the speed of your brain or mouth. This is why you see so many EI strategies that require you to take the time to write things down. It forces you to really examine your thoughts and opinions.

An analogy I like to use is to think of yourself driving your car into work. You are driving along at 55 miles an hour, so you miss all the little things that are lying on the side of the road. But if you rode your bike into work, you would see all the litter on the side of the road. If you walked, you would notice every cigarette butt, lost sock, tossed cup, and so on, lying on the side of the road. That's the difference between thinking your thoughts and talking about them versus writing them down.

Whenever I am coaching someone on their Emotional Quotient Assessment and I am trying to get them to slow down and really examine what they are doing, I always think of my old communication professors at Ohio State: "You never really understand what you are thinking until you write it down."

Neuroscience has proven them right.

DECISION-MAKING IS *EMOTIONAL*, NOT LOGICAL

It is important to understand that in order to make good decisions, we need both our logical brain (frontal lobes) and our emotional brain (amygdala).

Emotionally intelligent people are not devoid of emotions and ego. Humans use both their emotional and logical brains to make the best decisions they can.

Antonio Damasio, a behavioral neurologist, neuroscientist, and the director of the Brain and Creativity Institute at the University of Southern California, once had a patient named "Elliot." Elliot had, at one time, been very successful in both his personal and professional lives. He was happily married and held a high-ranking position in his law firm.[58] Unfortunately, Elliot developed a tumor about the size of a small orange right behind his forehead. Luckily, he was able to have the tumor surgically removed.[59]

Because of its location, however, his surgeons also had to sever the connections between his frontal lobes and his amygdala. As a result, Elliot's personality changed drastically.[60] After his surgery, Elliot lost his emotions. He no longer experienced anger, regret, sadness, frustration, or any other emotion that humans consistently display. He did not care when he was reprimanded at work. He could also no longer make decisions. In the end, he lost his prestigious position at the law firm, as well as his wife.[61]

Elliot then went to see Dr. Antonio Damasio. However, by the time he saw Dr. Damasio, Elliot was unemployed, broke, divorced, and living in a spare room at his brother's home.[62] When Elliot told Dr. Damasio about all the tragedies he had experienced since his surgery a few years earlier, Elliot showed no emotion at all. Dr. Damasio got more upset after hearing about Elliot's circumstances than Elliot did.[63]

Dr. Damasio tested Elliot and discovered that Elliot could still logically reason his way through problems just as he had always done in the past, and that he had not suffered any damage at all to his memory, his logic, his attention span, or any other cognitive ability. In other words, Elliot was just as "smart" as he had ever been.[64] However, because he no longer felt emotions, he got lost in minor details. He could not determine what was important when it came to solving problems. He lacked the ability to emotionally choose one potential solution over another and thus could not establish priorities. He could not attach value to any alternative he was considering. He felt neutral about everything. Elliot was now oblivious to how he felt about anything, including his own life.[65]

Elliot's inability to choose a course of action and make a decision was so bad that he could not decide when to schedule his next appointment with Dr. Damasio on his own. Elliot could reason through all the pros and cons of when it might be best to see Dr. Damasio again, but he could not choose between different available dates and times. Elliot had lost the ability to understand how he felt about any of these choices because he did not know how he felt about any of his options, thus rendering him unable to decide between them. Elliot had lost his ability to make decisions at the same time he lost his emotional system.[66] He had become Spock. Therefore, while humans use our logical brain to reason our way through various options, our emotional brain makes the final decision.[67]

CHAPTER 3

The Godfather Effect

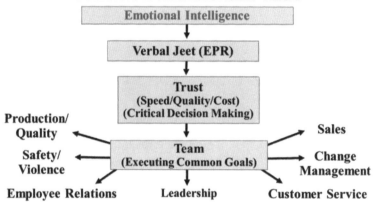

BUILDING A CHAMPIONSHIP TEAM

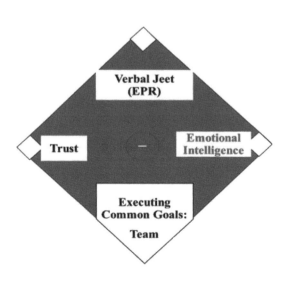

HAVING A HIGH IQ IS NOT ENOUGH

For years, we thought all you needed to be a great leader and successful in this world was to have a high IQ. That theory, of course, did not age out well. The first modern Intelligence Quotient test (IQ test) was developed in 1904 by French psychologists Alfred Binet and Théodore Simon. The French Ministry of Education asked Binet and Simon to develop a test to help the government determine if it was providing intellectually disabled children with sufficient education. The result was the Simon-Binet IQ test, which consisted of components such as logical reasoning, finding rhyming words, and naming objects, among others.[68]

Researchers soon tried to use this test to quantify someone's level of intelligence and separate average performers from excellent ones. Of course, using IQ scores to predict overall performance proved to be inaccurate. While IQ scores accurately predict one's level of intelligence in such areas as reading comprehension, writing, and arithmetic, there was not a positive correlation established between having a high IQ and being able to build trusting relationships. In fact, those with high IQs often proved to be very poor at managing their own behavior and getting along with others. Researchers also found that many of the people who received average scores on their IQ tests often surpassed those with higher IQ scores in both their personal and professional lives.[69]

Clearly, having a high IQ was not enough to predict future success.

Around this same time in the early 1900s, Edward Thorndike, a professor of psychology at Columbia University, developed his own theories of "adult learning." Thorndike stated that there were actually three main areas of intellectual development important for attaining one's goals.[70] He identified the first as "abstract intelligence," which is the ability to process and understand different concepts.[71] The second was "mechanical intelligence," which is the ability to handle physical objects.[72] Lastly, Thorndike claimed there was an area he called "social intelligence," which is the ability to handle human interaction.[73]

During World War I, the U.S. military wanted to be able to predict more accurately who would be most successful in the armed forces and who would not. They consulted with Thorndike to develop the Alpha and Beta versions of the test now known as the Armed Services Vocational Aptitude Battery (ASVAB). Thorndike developed a multiple-choice test that much more accurately assessed which individuals would be successful in the United States Armed Forces than an IQ test.[74] Over 100 years later, the ASVAB is still used by the U.S. Department of Defense to choose the best candidates. The ASVAB is administered at over 14,000 schools and Military Entrance Processing Stations (MEPS) across the country.[75]

Clearly, Thorndike was correct. Having a high IQ alone is not a good predictor of future success. Having a high level of social intelligence is much more important in predicting future success. Today, we refer to Thorndike's research when we talk about social intelligence as emotional intelligence. From research into social and emotional intelligence, Thorndike's theories have been proven correct many times over. Today, researchers claim that up to 90 percent of someone's success in areas such as personal achievement, goal attainment, happiness, and professional success can be attributed to one's level of emotional intelligence—not one's IQ.[76]

What an emotional quotient test is measuring can be broken down into two major categories: personal competence and social competence. Your personal competence represents your abilities in the areas of self-perception and self-management. Personal competence refers to your ability to be aware of what emotions you are experiencing and your ability to control them. Your social competence represents your abilities in the areas of interpersonal skills and decision-making skills. Social competence refers to your ability to understand other people's behavior and motives, as well as your ability to manage your various relationships. Unlike your IQ, which remains pretty much the same throughout adulthood, emotional intelligence is a very flexible skill that can be readily learned and increased through one's lifetime.

I have administered countless EQ assessments across the last two decades. I have then coached many of these individuals in how they can increase their level of emotional intelligence. Every time I coach anyone in this area, I am always asked the same question: Can someone really increase their level of EI?

My response it always the same: absolutely!

The only real question to ask is, "How much pain can you take?"

There is an old saying in sports: "pain is weakness leaving the body." The same is true for improving your EQ. Improving your EI is not for wimps. It is only for strong-willed and ferociously determined people. If you are not ready and able to address your weaknesses, you are not prepared. You have to face your inadequacies, as painful as they are to admit, and then you must attack them. You have to listen to the advice you get, apply it, and change the way you look at yourself and the way you treat others. You must transform yourself and that is never easy.

In other words, the degree to which you will improve is directly related to how much pain you can take.

A few years ago, the *Harvard Business Review* addressed this issue of why alpha males need coaching and why their emotional intelligence tends to be so low in "Coaching the Alpha Male," by Eddie Erlandson and Kate Ludeman. This article concluded that many alpha males in particular desperately need coaching because their emotional intelligence tends to be very low.[77] Their "macho," "John Wayne" self-image tells them that they always need to be the one with the answer and they need to be "tough." This self-image will often end in disaster.

I often see instances where this article is spot-on. In fact, I have coached many executive men in powerful positions who thought they were tough. Many of them were not. They were weak and could not take the pain. They could not evolve from their basic caveman state into a strong, self-confident person who can relate to others and not just themselves. They were in reality emotional children.

Unfortunately, our society values a "grab them by the nose" mentality. We love John Wayne's persona in the movies--kill them and don't compromise. We love to see Simon Cowell insult someone until they cry. Of course, in real life, such a person would drive an organization into the ground.

Whenever you are dealing with humans, you have to always remember that you are dealing with the most fickle, emotional, and dangerous animal on the planet. If you offend a human, they will get you back. Humans are emotional animals who are motivated by their self-esteem, which can kick into gear in about 17,000ths of a second. If you treat people like Simon Cowell does in the real world, you will most likely get employees who will find some way to retaliate the first second they think they can get away with it. Remember, according to OSHA, over 38,000 physical assaults occur every week in American workplaces. That is two million physical assaults per year. Also remember OSHA's report that the U.S. sees an average of about two workplace homicides each workday.

Sadly, our society does not value great leaders such as Henry David Thoreau, although his theory of civil disobedience changed the world. Why? Because he was against war. He wasn't a cowboy and never kicked anyone's butt.

I have thought for a long time as to who the best and most recognizable role model for the ultimate emotionally intelligent communicator could be. In the past, I used Abraham Lincoln. He was the master of EI. He surrounded himself with the brightest minds of his time for his cabinet, even though many were his rivals and thought they could do a better job than he was as president. Doris Kearns Goodwin even wrote a book, *Team of Rivals: The Political Genius of Abraham Lincoln*, on Lincoln's ability to put his ego and emotions aside in order to focus on the best advice he could get, even though it was often contrary to what he wanted to do. However, Lincoln is so revered today that he almost loses his humanity and as a result, he has become hard to identify with for many people.

I then thought of Yoda, from *Star Wars*.

First, I like Yoda because he is short and bald. However, he is also the most powerful Jedi in the universe because of his great control over his own mind. Unfortunately, many people do not relate to *Star Wars*. (Which is just sad. If most people were Jedi Knights, the Force would already be with them and they would already have the essential skills of being an emotionally intelligent communicator, and we would not be having this discussion right now. But, I digress.)

I then thought of Professor Albus Dumbledore from the *Harry Potter* series. However, a lot of older folks might not get that reference right away.

I then thought of the role model I used years ago to prep clients for deposition and cross examination: The Godfather, Don Vito Corleone. He is perfect, I mean, once you get past all of the killing, gambling, prostitution, loan sharking, and so on. But if you can just overlook all of the felonies he commits on a daily basis, Marlon Brando's *Godfather* character, Don Vito Corleone, makes an excellent role model for emotional intelligence.

Don Corleone keeps his cool. He adopted a slow, methodical decision-making process that allows him to keep his emotions in check, which makes him able to listen more than he talks. He doesn't let others know what he is thinking until he wants them to know and avoids making rash decisions by not rushing to think through decisions. He can manage his behavior to fit what he needs to do at any given time. He has tremendous empathy for those around him, and because of that, he is able to build great relationships with those on his team. He builds a trusting environment of people who are willing to die and kill for him. He does not react emotionally and take revenge on his enemies when it will hurt his ability to reach his ultimate goals. He is able to keep his emotions in check and logically deal with his enemies—even after they killed his oldest son, Sonny, and tried to also kill him.

For example, Don Corleone forgives the people who killed Sonny when he needs their help to bring his youngest son back from Sicily, where he is in hiding for killing a guy in New York. Not only that, he hugs and kisses the man who had his oldest son killed. Most parents can certainly understand the tremendous emotional control someone would have to possess in order to forgive—much less hug—anyone who has harmed, much less killed, one of their children. It is almost super-human. However, Don Corleone understands what he must do in order to protect his youngest son, Michael. In order to attain his greater goal, logic wins out over emotions.

Don Corleone would have made a great professional poker player.

I also always think of emotional intelligence when I think of my beloved Ohio State Buckeyes during football season. (Go Bucks!)

Whenever a Buckeye jumps offside, I think, "Okay, who got into your head? What caused you to lose your focus? Can't you count to three?" Whenever a receiver runs the wrong route, I think, "Why is your head not in the game? Who got inside your head?"

Perhaps one of the worst instances of losing your cool as a Buckeye fan was in 2013 when Marcus Hall, a starting offensive lineman for Ohio State, lost it. During "The Game" between Michigan and Ohio State—the greatest rivalry game in all of sports according to *Sports Illustrated*—a fight broke out right at the beginning between opposing players. Unfortunately, Marcus Hall could not control his emotions and he jumped into the brawl. As a result, he was ejected from "The Game."

Marcus was a senior. This was his last Michigan versus Ohio State game.

Moreover, Marcus was a starting offensive lineman, which is one of the most important positions on the entire team. And he could not keep his cool long enough to keep from getting thrown out of "The Game." Sitting at home watching "The Game," I could not believe what I was seeing. So, my question was, à la Red Forman: "What kind of a dumbass are you?"

Then, just to show how immature we Buckeyes can be, Marcus flipped off the entire Michigan fan base at Michigan Stadium, or the "Big House," as he left the field.

Again: you can't do anything if you do not have control over yourself.

I used to love it when I had to cross examine or depose someone who was an emotional child. I could tell right where their weaknesses were, and it always had something to do with their ego. All I had to do was challenge them in one of their sensitive areas. Within a few minutes, they would crack. I could immediately tell when I hit a vital area. They told me everything I needed to know. Their eyes would squint ever so slightly. Their eyebrows would furrow. They would adjust their shoulders, subconsciously getting ready to fight. They would then take deeper breaths because their blood was starting to go to the muscles in their arms, legs, and lungs. They would start to raise their voice. They would sweat. Their lips would purse.

In my mind, I was smiling and thinking, "Yes! That is their kryptonite! I've got this egomaniac on the ropes … right where I want them."

My favorites were the "Human Thermometers." With these people, their necks first start to turn red. This red rash would then quickly move up to their chin line and then onto their cheeks. When the red rash finally reached their eyes, they would explode. At that point, I knew I had won; if you cannot control yourself, then others will control you.

I always wondered why rattling important people was so easy. Didn't they know what I was doing? Of course, they did. Their lawyer surely had prepped them. However, there is nothing you can do with an emotional child if they are not tough enough to take the pain of transformation.

As I mentioned earlier, Eddie Erlandson and Kate Ludeman's article, "Coaching the Alpha Male," addressed the issue of why alpha males need more coaching than most people and why their emotional intelligence tends to be so much lower than others.

They explain that most Alphas reach the top because they do not shy away from responsibility. They gravitate towards it. Most people, on the other hand, feel overwhelmed whenever they have to make important decisions. They choke. Alphas instead feel distress when they are not the one making the decision. Being in control gives them a rush of adrenaline. You need Alpha leaders because most people don't want to be doing that job.

Unfortunately, most Alphas learn at an early age that most people do not like making important decisions. Alphas also learn that they probably really are smarter than most people. As a result, they become very impatient and undervalue the opinions of others. They tend to look down on people who don't think like them or act like them. Alphas also tend to think they are experts in everything. Because they have always had to make many different kinds of decisions, usually very quickly, they tend to believe they can do that on most any topic, largely because relying on their gut instincts has gotten them this far.

Of course, this is not true. As one moves up in the corporate ladder, decisions become more and more complicated and more data is required to make sound decisions. Therefore, it is only a matter of time until they make a grave mistake. When the day comes when they are wrong, they cannot admit their mistake. They tend to think that admitting a mistake means they are showing a lack of leadership and weakness.

Alphas also rely on their logical brains too much. Many Alphas think that every problem has a logical answer, which clearly is not true because humans are emotional animals. They think that acknowledging the feelings and emotions of others is just "fuzzy, feel-good stuff" and has no place in business. Human emotions only get in the way of getting the job done and because of this they tend to look down on those who express their emotions, even though they completely overlook their own angry outbursts and tirades. In the end, the more an Alpha achieves, the more pressure they feel and the more pronounced their faults can become.

In other words, as a general rule, they become emotional children who alienate others.

Alphas act more like Sonny Corleone: they are rash, emotional, and explosive. The instant gratification they get by taking revenge on their enemies, or anyone who disagrees with them, takes precedent over making logical decisions that benefit their organization. All of these uncontrolled emotional responses hurt their organization and may later result in their own "corporate capital punishment."

Whenever I administer emotional quotient (EQ) assessments to my clients, I immediately think of "Coaching the Alpha Male." It is very clear from the test scores that most people in positions of power have great abilities in such areas as assertiveness, independence, and problem-solving because our culture values these traits. Our common lore says that these are all vital if you are going to be a strong leader. However, these same leaders typically do not score well in such areas as empathy, emotional self-awareness, and interpersonal relationships because our society does not place as much value on these traits.

According to Bradberry and Greaves, only 36 percent of the people you know on average are able to accurately identify the emotions they are experiencing. This is a major roadblock to our success personally and professionally. If you cannot recognize an emotion as it arises, you will not be able to control it. It will control you. Amazingly, this means that two-thirds of us are being actively controlled by our emotions, which places everyone in a very dangerous situation.[78]

The daily emotional distresses we experience often render us unable to resolve the interpersonal conflict we encounter. On average, more than 70 percent of everyone you know cannot effectively handle the stress they are feeling, which includes the ever-changing situations they are experiencing at work.[79] Because of our inability to confront our emotions head-on, most of us retreat from conflicts at work and become passive-aggressive, which in turn will kill your relationships and your career, as we will discuss later in these materials.

In the end, trust dies, as does any hope of building a team. What effect does this have on your organization?

According to researchers Dr. Travis Bradberry and Dr. Jean Greaves, only 15 percent of employees they surveyed feel they are treated with respect and valued by their employer. Consequently, four out of every five people would leave their current job if they were offered a similar job with similar pay somewhere else.[80] Unfortunately, when someone's job title increases, the person's level of EI tends to drop dramatically. Middle managers actually tend to have the highest level of EI in the organization because they still have several people holding them accountable. They know they will have to justify their actions to someone. However, once someone is promoted above middle management, their emotional scores tend to drop like a rock. CEOs often have the lowest EI scores in the organization because there is no one to correct them or hold them accountable in any significant way.[81] When people are afraid to disagree with them, they tend to think they are correct about everything. In the end, they become "God."

They do not act like Don Vito Corleone.

EI: BALANCING OUR EGOS AND EMOTIONS

When I teach this subject in a seminar, I will inevitably be asked the question: "So, if I become upset or angry, then I'm an emotional child?"

No, that is not the case at all.

Becoming an emotionally intelligent person does not mean that you have eliminated your emotions or your ego. You are human, and your emotions and ego are very important to your ability to thrive as a human being. Our emotions and our egos are good things when we remain in control of them—not the other way around.

I will then ask the audience how many of them got to the seminar in a car. Of course, most of the hands go up. I will then ask them if a car is a good thing. The audience will then always respond with a resounding "Yes."

To that, I will ask, "But what if you can't control it?"

The audience will think for a minute before they get it.

Just like a car, or anything else for that matter, emotions and ego are good things only if we can control them.

I will then ask the audience, "Don't you want people with healthy egos, people who are self-confident and are good at what they do coming into work every day?"

The audience will respond, "Yes, of course we do."

"But what if you cannot control that ego? Now you have Enron."

I will then ask the audience, "And don't you want people with emotions who like their job walking into work every day on the balls of their feet?"

The audience will then respond, "Sure, that is high morale."

"But what if you cannot control your emotions? Now you're more likely to experience workplace violence and aggression. Now you have a tragedy."

Being an emotionally intelligent person does not mean that you do not have emotions or an ego. Emotionally intelligent people do not become Spock. Quite the contrary. They are still human beings, but they use their EI skills to remain in control of their emotions and ego. Emotions and ego drive our passions and give us confidence. Without passion and self-confidence, we become ineffective. Both are vital to our success and happiness. However, the emotionally intelligent person is able to keep the two worlds of emotions/ego and logic in balance with each other.

Again, a car is a good thing, but not if you cannot control it. Being an emotionally intelligent person fundamentally means you are able to control your ego and emotions. They do not control you.

THE SEVEN PITFALLS OF LOW EMOTIONAL INTELLIGENCE

Emotional children are all around us to one degree or another. It is a constant challenge for the human animal to keep their ego and emotions in check. Because our natural instinct is fight-or-flight, we are not wired to be emotionally intelligent communicators. So, how do you spot an emotional child?

The greatest telltales that you are dealing with an emotional child are as follows:

1. They are unable to control their emotions and ego.
    They cannot communicate in conflict situations due to their uncontrolled emotions. So, they either become passive-aggressive "Retreaters" who run away when conflict arises, and then stab others in the back later, or they attack their team mates. Either way, the conflict either gets suppressed or escalated but it does not get resolved. As a result of their

reactionary approach to conflict, they destroy trust and others clam up around them. Because of this, they are not able to gather all of the crucial facts needed to engage in real critical decision-making.

2. They dismiss any opinions that disagree with their own.
   They base their decisions and reactions on ego and emotion, not on logic. They rush to judgment without investigating the facts. Actually, for these people, the facts only get in the way of a good opinion. They cannot admit their own mistakes and will not accept feedback, and thus they cannot improve. When things go wrong, they blame everyone else rather than trying to correct the situation. They adopt a "my way or the highway" mentality, and as a result, these emotional children do not gather and examine all of the pertinent facts needed to make an informed decision. In the end, critical decision-making becomes unachievable.

3. They reward bootlickers.
   People who tell them what they want to hear are rewarded. They love bootlickers, so they surround themselves with them. Groupthink becomes the norm, with disastrous results. Dissenters are punished and shunned.

4. They have little or no empathy for others.
   They are very self-centered. They are unable to see the perspective of others, and they don't care. Their perspective is the only one that matters. They try to manipulate others for their own gain. Due to their distrustful and devious nature, they are not able to build trusting relationships with others. It is truly is not safe to disagree with them.

5. They are mind-blind.
   They do not realize the destructive impact they have on others, and/or they don't care. They walk around the organization like Pepé Le Pew. They think they smell great, but they leave a trail of stink behind them that makes most people cringe.

6. They micromanage others.
   They believe no one can do anything as well as they can, so they build very little trust. They also fail to develop their people and increase their

abilities. In the end, they take on everything and become overworked and bitter. They become their own martyrs.

7. They either suppress or escalate conflict, but they do not resolve it. As a result, conflicts simply get worse.

EMOTIONAL CHILD CHECKLIST

_____ Cannot control their emotions and ego

_____ Dismiss any opinions that disagree with their own

_____ Reward bootlickers

_____ Little or no empathy for others

_____ Mind blind

_____ Micromanage others

_____ They either suppress or escalate conflict, but they do not resolve it

---

WHAT IS AN "ASSHOLE"?

When I was conducting this program for a client, I made it clear that if you show me an emotional child, I will show you someone who is intolerant of others.

What does it mean to be "intolerant?" An intolerant person is someone who will persecute you because you are different, which includes disagreeing with them. In other words, if you disagree with an intolerant person, they will get you. At that point, I had someone in the audience shout out, "You mean they're an asshole!"

Of course, everyone laughed, including me. "Why do you say that?" I asked.

"That's the book we're all reading right now," he said.

I looked at him and very intelligently asked, "Huh?"

He then showed me the book, *Assholes: A Theory* by Aaron James. No, he wasn't kidding. The entire management team was reading it, and they loved it.

"Yeah," he said. "What you are describing is an 'asshole.'"

They gave me a copy of the book. I read it—and I loved it! It is a very good book, but it uses very different terms than the usual emotional intelligence books I am used to reading. It dawned on me: no one is going to call you an emotional child.

They are going to call you an "asshole."

That is about as real world as it gets. We see them all around us, and readily identify them, every day of our lives. I went on Amazon and searched for these types of books. What I found astonished me. There are actually several books on this topic of being an asshole: *Assholes; The No Asshole Rule: Building a Civilized Workplace and Surviving One That Isn't; Dear Asshole;* and *Asshole: How I Got Rich & Happy by Not Giving a Damn About Anyone & How You Can, Too.*

The common theme that runs through many of these books is that an asshole is someone who believes they are more important than everyone else.

Someone cuts you off in traffic. Why? Because their need to get to where they are going is much more important than your need to get to where you are going. Someone yells at you, or they play the role of a passive-aggressive and stab you in the back later for disagreeing with them on a highly emotional topic. Why? Because their need to be right is much more important than your opinion, regardless of the facts. Someone at work lies and blames you for a mistake that is not your fault. Why? Because their need to look good is much more important than your need to look good. (Although I loved the real-world application, I did not love it enough to change the title of this book.)

My client was quite right. In the real world, no one will say you are an emotional child. They will call you an asshole, and no one wants that.

IT ALL BEGINS WITH EMOTIONAL INTELLIGENCE

The reason why so many of the different programs corporate America puts into place each year fail is simple. It's because we spend so much time planning how to implement and maintain the program itself that we ignore the most important factor of all: we are trying to implement a good program with emotional children. In short, if you do not have emotionally intelligent people working with you, none of your programs that require a sharing of ideas will work. Important programs affected by the lack of emotional intelligence include:

- **Safety Programs** fail because people do not want to get into trouble for bringing up an issue that will be unpopular, so they will not communicate with each other. Many employees are intimidated by supervisors who manage like they are on an ego trip, so employees do not talk when they break a safety rule or cause an accident for fear of getting in trouble. Also, most people have terrible listening skills, largely because they only care about their own opinion, so messages are not received correctly. As a result, no one speaks and no one listens, and more of the same types of accidents occur again and again.

- **Employee Relations Programs** fail because managers and employees will alienate one another in order to gain a position of power over the other so they can boost their fragile egos. Supervisors and their employees begin to struggle for power in an effort to bully each other, and the goal of having a successful organization falls by the wayside. The real goal of the organization now becomes to "stick it to you." Employees, management, and labor alike begin to sabotage each other at the expense of the organization's success. Emotions take over to the point where labor and management begin to hate each other. Grievances rise, production falls off, and quality drops. In many of these situations, the union comes in and organizes the company's employees—and often rightfully so.

- **Teambuilding Programs** fail because trust is destroyed. The sense of being a team fails because speaking up to correct a problem could make someone look bad and the social leaders will punish anyone who might embarrass them. Groupthink becomes the norm.

- **Change Management Programs** fail because the egos of emotional children are so fragile that they cannot stand the thought of failure. They are afraid to fail and thus will continually resist any organizational changes.

- **Leadership** also fails because too many emotional children assume positions of power in order to go on their own personal ego trip, and so they will kill the messenger whenever anyone disagrees with their ideas.

Leaders begin to think they are too good to eat with subordinates. Private parking is necessary because they view themselves as being more important than their workers, and thus "need" a spot. Relationships fall apart, distrust between management and labor grows, production levels and quality start to drop, the number of employees missing work rises, grievances increase, and so on.

- **Production** and **Quality** drop because front line employees are so frustrated from being bullied that they don't care as much about the company anymore and because their emotions are running the show, they forget about their direct self-interest in the company's success. Apathy becomes the norm. Later, some employees will even sabotage the company's product or steal from the company in order to create a sense of equity in the situation. Rather than helping the organization succeed, the primary goal of most people is to "stick it to the management."

- **Workplace Violence** increases because people finally snap. Because emotional children are constantly trying to show everyone how important they are, they bully others to move up in the pecking order. The increased bullying from these people finally reaches its breaking point when the staplers and coffee cups go flying.

- **Customer Service** has a decrease in quality because the employees who have to deal with upset or difficult customers are not able to control their egos and emotions, and thus escalate these situations rather than diffuse them. It is simply hypocritical for supervisors to tell employees that they have to give superior customer service to the customers when they treat their employees like dirt. This dichotomy never goes unnoticed.

- **Sales** drop because salespeople cannot build effective relationships with clients and cannot read the verbal and nonverbal cues sent by customers regarding what they really want. They also will not listen to advice that will help them improve.

- And so on, and so on, and so on…

In other words, no other program you will ever adopt in your organization will have as much impact on each of these nine vital areas of your business than insisting on having people act with emotional intelligence. The studies in this area are overwhelmingly clear in saying that nothing good happens in your organization if you cannot act like the bigger person!

As we progress in our careers, the ability to grow our emotional intelligence so we can use our Verbal Jeet Skills (EPR = Empathic Listening, Parroting, and "Rewards") to resolve conflict and build trust with others becomes more and more critical. (We will address our Verbal Jeet Skills later in these materials.)

The studies supporting this position are overwhelming:

- Technical expertise helps you get your job. However, it is your level of emotional intelligence that makes you a "star performer." Being able to build relationships and work with others makes you a success and gets you promoted, not your technical skills. IQ contributes only 4–10 percent toward a leader's success. The higher someone rises in an organization or in their career, the more impact that person's emotional intelligence has on determining their success. Oftentimes, one's level of emotional intelligence will contribute as much as 90 percent of a person's success.[82]
- One study of more than 300 top-level executives from 15 global companies showed that high emotional intelligence skills was the factor that separated top performers from average ones.[83]
- In another study, divisional leaders who demonstrated high levels of emotional intelligence surpassed their revenue targets by a margin of 15–20 percent. However, those who had lower levels of emotional intelligence underperformed compared to their peers by almost 20 percent.[84]
- At MetLife, sales agents who scored low in emotional intelligence sold an average of $54,000 in product each year. Alternatively, those sales agents who scored high in emotional intelligence had an annual sales average of $114,000.[85]
- A large beverage firm used its standard hiring methods to select divisional presidents, which did not assess the applicant's emotional intelligence abilities. 50 percent of those applicants who were hired left the company within the first two years, mostly because of poor performance. The loss from these hiring mistakes cost the company an estimated $4 million. When the company started selecting divisional presidents based on their level of emotional intelligence, only 6 percent left in their first two years.[86]

- Research conducted by the Center for Creative Leadership has found that the primary reason executives fail in their careers is due to a lack of emotional intelligence. The three primary causes for this failure are their inability to handle change, not being able to work well on a team, and their poor interpersonal relations with others.[87]

In short, success is emotional intelligence.

EMOTIONAL INTELLIGENCE IS NOT A "NEW" PROGRAM

Implementing emotional intelligence throughout your organization or into your lifestyle does not mean that you are simply following a fad diet or a new flavor of the month. Instead, building the emotional intelligence of your people allows you to do what you are already doing better. Emotional intelligence teaches you how to conduct yourself like an emotionally mature person, which means you are better able to remain in control of your ego and emotions, work cooperatively with other people, and build relationships with others. It is a lifestyle that gives you more control over your own well-being. If this does not happen, then nothing works. You simply cannot implement successful programs with emotional children.

For example, I once had a client who worked in human resources. She wanted to implement a new emotional intelligence program in her organization but wanted to wait until after negotiations with the union were completed. I stopped for a minute, then asked her, "Why? Do you want your negotiations to be as difficult as possible?"

I asked her the following questions:

- How productive do you think your negotiations are going to be if you have emotional children on your team?
- Don't you want them to keep their cool during negotiations?
- Shouldn't they listen more than they talk?
- Do you want them to make logical decisions or emotional ones?
- Don't you want to build trust amongst the members of your negotiating team?
- Don't you want your negotiating team to understand people on the other side—both their behaviors and their motives?

Again, becoming an emotionally intelligent communicator improves upon everything you are already doing. Unfortunately, she was trying to implement all of her programs with emotional three-year-olds on her team, which will not end well.

I often talk to managers and CEOs who are desperately trying to find ways to make their various programs become more successful. They examine and re-examine how their program was designed and how it was implemented. All too often, the flaw was not in the design of the program, nor was it in the plan's implementation. They simply tried to implement a good plan with emotional children who were incapable of handling it.

Whenever I encounter these situations, I ask the CEO if the company wants:

- to build a good team?
- higher quality, higher production, and lower waste?
- better customer service?
- better relationships between management and labor?
- to be better equipped to diffuse situations rather than escalate them?
- lower turnover?
- to reduce its chance of workplace violence?
- to prevent illegal harassment and EEO claims?

In short, none of your programs will work if you try implementing them with emotional children. Most anyone who has spent any time in the real world has worked with "toddlers" who ruin everything for everybody. They understand how destructive these bullies can be to anyone who has ever encountered them. In short, if you cannot act like the bigger person, game over. Nothing good will happen.

QUANTIFYING EMOTIONAL INTELLIGENCE

In his book, *Managing in a Time of Great Change*, Peter Drucker said that "being an educated person is no longer enough. We have to … get into competencies … do you like pressure? … can you be steady? … empathy is a practical competence." What he is talking about is the very essence of emotional intelligence.

There are five traits, or skills, that have been identified and widely accepted as having the most influence over our emotional intelligence score. These factors are today referred to as the "Big Five:"

• Self-perception skills
• Self-expression skills
• Interpersonal skills
• Decision-making skills
• Stress management skills

Of course, each of these Big Five skills encompass other factors that are measured to give the person their overall score for each Big Five skill. Personally, I use the EQ-i 2.0® assessment from Multi-Health Systems Inc. (MHS). The EQ-i 2.0® assessment requires a sixth to seventh grade reading level, includes 133 assessment questions, has a five-point response scale (1 being never/rarely, 3 being sometimes, and 5 being always/almost always), takes about 20–30 minutes to complete, and has an average score of 100—the same as an IQ test.

Having a high EQ means that you are able to gain better control over your ego and emotions, which will result in being more effective personally and socially. As we have already discussed, our emotional system is much faster than our logical system; our thoughts race through our brains at an astonishing 268 miles per hour, which is why we sometimes say really stupid things, catch ourselves, and say something like, "That really sounded better in my head." Attaining and maintaining a high EQ is consequently the hardest thing any of us will ever do because it works against our human nature.

In the following section, you will see the Big Five categories that comprise the EQ assessment and learn self-help strategies for each area, including ones that force you to slow down your thinking. Other strategies include bouncing ideas off of a sounding board, talking things over with a mentor, talking to yourself out loud, meditation, and so on. On the following pages, you will see the Big Five skills of the Emotional Quotient Inventory test, as well as individual subset information about each skill and various self-help strategies.

Self-Perception Skills

Self-Regard: You respect and accept yourself; you are confident.

Self-Actualization: You can pursue meaning and self-improvement in your life. You have the drive to set and achieve personal goals.

Emotional Self-Awareness: Being aware of and understanding one's emotions.

Possible Strategies for Improvement

- Focus on and record successes. Reward yourself.
- Realize your strengths and be aware of weaknesses, but do not obsess over them. Write them down. Take your time. Set plans and goals for improving weaknesses. Take charge.
- Set goals for learning new skills and acquiring new knowledge. Benchmark successes.
- Take time to reflect. Meditate. Think about what you are dealing with and why you react the way you do. Self-control and awareness is the key.
- Articulate what bothers you by actually saying it out loud. Consciously ask yourself, "Why did I react or feel that way?" after an intense interaction. Maybe you should record yourself and listen to the playback later.
- Get a sounding board or mentor to bounce ideas off.
- Examine where you are in life and where you want to be, both privately and professionally. Set goals to get where you want to be, establish a realistic plan, and then start.
- Monitor progress frequently (e.g., weekly or monthly).
- Keep goals realistic. "What can I really do?" Reassess if necessary.
- Increase social interactions to both express yourself and listen to others' feelings and thoughts.
- Keep a diary or journal and record these emotions and feelings. (*Remember:* you never really understand something until you write it down.)
- Identify your hot spots and what triggers your anger.

Self-Expression Skills

Emotional Expression: Constructively expressing your emotions.

Assertiveness: Communicating feelings and beliefs in an inoffensive way.

Independence: Self-directed. Free from emotional dependency.

Possible Strategies for Improvement

- Adjust your expectations.
- Get a sounding board. Express your emotions and ask for feedback.
- Talk things out loud and voice your emotions to yourself. Using a recorder and listening to the playback can be useful.
- Practice initializing a conversation strategically to keep others off the defensive. Use your Verbal Jeet (EPR) Skills to resolve conflicts.
- Keep a diary or journal. Write down your emotions, then examine and discuss them with yourself or a sounding board.
- Do not retreat or attack in high stakes situations. Practice using your Verbal Jeet (EPR) Skills to resolve conflicts with people you trust.
- Build trust with others by creating a space where it is safe to disagree with you by using your Verbal Jeet (EPR) Skills to resolve conflicts.
- Get a mentor to help and oversee your progress.
- Increase your skills and knowledge to build confidence. Audiobooks from your local public library are great for this.
- Recognize your strengths and weaknesses. Lean into your strengths and improve your weaknesses.
- Practice before you go into a difficult conversation with someone. Ask someone to role play difficult conversations with you. Don't go in cold.

Interpersonal Skills

Interpersonal Relationship: You establish mutually satisfying relationships with others.

Empathy: Being aware of and understanding how others feel.

Social Responsibility: You have a social conscience and want to help others. You identify with and are part of your social group.

Possible Strategies for Improvement
- Make sure to spend time with others to build relationships. Set this as a priority.
- Use your Verbal Jeet (EPR) Skills to resolve conflicts in critical, high-stakes situations.
- Adopt empathic listening as a specific practice. (Use your EPR skills.) Remember Stephen Covey: "seek first to understand, then seek to be understood." Ask the other person, "How do you see this?"
- Build trust. That means you must show to others that it is okay to disagree with you.
- Practice and learn to read the nonverbal cues of others, specifically facial expressions. (To learn more about reading such nonverbal cues, just go to www.paulekman.com.)
- Expose yourself to others with very different points of view and backgrounds and listen. Do not react defensively.
- Get a sounding board. Ask what impact your actions are having on others.
- Take part in more group activities, either at work or in your private life.
- Adopt certain goals that require group projects.

Decision-Making Skills

Problem–Solving: You are able to find effective solutions when emotions are involved.

Reality Testing: You can remain objective and see things the way they really are.

Impulse Control: Resist or delay the impulse to act.

Possible Strategies for Improvement
- Get a mentor or a sounding board to practice thorough analysis or decision-making. Get feedback on your analysis. Ask yourself what you are not seeing.
- Participate in brainstorming sessions and listen.
- Educate yourself in cost/benefit analysis and critical decision-making. You can always purchase courses on these skills on Amazon, Audible, and from

The Great Courses. Learning more in these areas can help you use logic over emotion.

- Write down your analysis of problems and be critical!
- Seek multiple sources of information for different points of view on various issues. Again, do not react emotionally. Slow down and think.
- Never categorize the other side as stupid. Their values differ and they might make you look foolish.
- Get a devil's advocate to challenge you. Practice responses for when someone disagrees with you and maybe insults you. If you cannot control yourself in role playing or practice situations, you will surely fail in real-life situations.
- Develop a waiting strategy such as waiting 24–72 hours before replying to an insulting email, etc.
- Know your weaknesses and then stop and focus on another activity to control bad impulses. Know when to hold! Whenever you are in doubt—stop!
- Adopt procedures that require the input of others and a more methodical process on your part.

Stress Management Skills

Flexibility: Coping with and adapting to change in one's daily life.
Stress Tolerance: Effectively and constructively managing one's emotions under stress.
Optimism: Having a positive outlook and looking at the brighter side of life.

Possible Strategies for Improvement
- Plan, plan, and plan some more so you will be able to revert to a Plan B or even a Plan C when things go wrong. The more control you feel you have over things, the less stress you will typically experience.
- Break projects into small parts. This gives you more control and makes life more manageable.
- Make sure you set goals that are attainable, then appreciate successes.

- Reflect on past experiences when circumstances change and get advice. Expect change.
- Know your limits and pet peeves. Plan to avoid such situations and do not wait to ask for help.
- Use your time effectively. Log your time.
- Prioritize. Not everything is important.
- Before you react emotionally, stop and think.
- Recognize automatic negative thoughts (ANTS), then slow down and reason your way through them. We all have ANTS because we are all human. Our fears take us right to the negative in 17,000ths of a second. However, most ANTS are not real. They are your subconscious fears turning up in your head. Slow down and reason your way through each one. Don't let them rule your mind.
- Focus on solutions rather than adopting a "woe is me" mentality.
- Stay away from problem people who infest your lives. They transmit their negative emotions to you and drag you down with them.

What Is Happiness? You appreciate where you are in life. You appreciate those people around you. You can relax and enjoy yourself.

Possible Strategies for Improvement
- Track successes and take time to celebrate.
- Identify the activities you really enjoy and do them.
- Balance your work and private life as much as possible and recognize the pleasurable aspects of your work.
- Set private and professional goals and track your progress.
- Develop meaningful relationships everywhere.

READING AN EQ ASSESSMENT

In reading an emotional intelligence assessment, you first look at the high scores and then look at the low scores. You want all of your scores to be within 10 points of one another because otherwise, your skills will not balance one another out and thus your strengths will actually become weaknesses. It is not bad to get a high score in assertiveness unless you also happen to get a very low score in empathy, because the lack of empathy will not keep the assertiveness in check. You will come across as overbearing and hard to get along with from your peers and superiors.

Reading an EQ assessment is a lot like sliding down a banister. You want to choose a banister that is as even and smooth as possible. Any bumps or spikes that project up too far would get your attention in a nuclear kind of way when you hit them. When you look at your EQ scores, you need to ask yourself if this is a banister you would like to slide down.

You read an EQ test just like you would read an IQ test. A score of 100 is average. Anything above that is above average and anything below 100 is below average. Therefore, just like an IQ test, you want all of your EQ scores to be at least 100. An EQ assessment gives you a picture of a person's strengths and weaknesses on the 15 points addressed in the test. The best way to understand how such scores are quantified is to review a few real-life examples. All of the following have been provided with permission from MHS.

ED

Ed was sent to me because he was failing in his job. He was seen as a great go-getter, but he was also ticking off his subordinates and superiors, as well as the Board of Directors. His job was in jeopardy. So, I tested Ed's EQ.

As you can see, Ed scored very well on "assertiveness" (123) and "independence" (124). That actually put him in the superior range for these skills. Ed truly was a real go-getter with a forceful personality. However, his scores on "interpersonal relationships" (86) and "empathy" (83) were very low. When it came to "interpersonal relationships" and "empathy," Ed was Forrest Gump. In short, he simply did not value building relationships with other people. He believed trampling over others was acceptable if it got him to his immediate goal. He had adopted a Simon Cowell-esque approach to business.

Ed believed achieving his goal was more important than building relationships with others. In fact, Ed specifically told me that he was proud of the fact that his peers called him an "asshole."

ED's EQ-i 2.0 ASSESSMENT

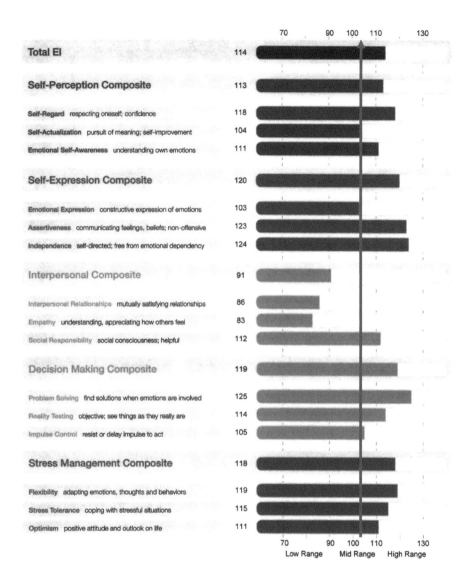

"Sometimes, you just have to be an asshole to get things done right," Ed told me.

Ed's approach does work for the immediate project or problem at hand. Being an asshole to other people can be effective, but only in the short term. In the long run, it will kill your team's morale. What Ed did not think through was that he would also have to work with these same people on the next project. As a result, even though he had never missed a deadline, he was failing in his job because he was alienating everyone around him. Some employees said if they had to work with Ed again, they would quit.

At first, Ed thought his scores were great. He was high on such scores as assertiveness, independence, and problem-solving—all of the scores he valued. Because Ed did not value such traits as interpersonal relationships and empathy, he did not see an issue with having below average scores in those areas.

"That is just fuzzy, feel-good garbage," Ed told me. "I don't kiss up to anybody."

Obviously, we had a lot of work to do. I then asked Ed if he knew why I was there and why he was asked to take this test.

"It's just a bunch of politics," he replied. "Someone pitched a fit so I have to take this test, talk to you, and do some penitence."

"No," I told him. "I am the only thing standing between you and the door."

Ed stared at me incredulously.

I then told him, "Ed, my job is to try and help you."

Again, Ed just looked at me in bewilderment.

"I am not here to put you through some elementary exercises. I am here to see if you can improve. Your superiors want to see real improvement, not just lip service. I believe you are very skilled technically at your job, but you leave a trail of upset people behind you wherever you go. People just don't want to work with you."

"So, I should just start kissing everybody's butt?" he retorted.

I leaned back and just looked at Ed for a few seconds.

"Do you talk to other people here the way you are talking to me right now?" I asked. "Because if you do, I am not so sure 'trust' can be rebuilt with your fellow employees. You are going to have to work really hard to turn your reputation around here. I mean, people usually put on their best face when they have to come and see me. If this is your best face, I'm afraid you're in a lot of trouble."

"You know, I really don't have to take this. I can leave anytime I want and get another job," he said. I opened his file.

"I'm sure you can. Actually, I see you change jobs quite frequently. This is your seventh job in 20 years." I leaned back in my chair again and looked at him. "That's kind of a lot."

Now Ed glared at me.

"You know, I am here to try and help you. You clearly have issues in building relationships and seeing other people's points of view. It's clear that you have great strengths, but because you don't have these other skills, you are off-balance. Your scores are not within 10 points of each other, so they do not balance each other out. The only question I have for you in determining if you are going to improve is this: how much pain can you take?"

I told Ed, "It is tough to hear that your career is going nowhere because of the way you are reacting to other people. It is even tougher to hear that you need to work on these personal skills, but that is clearly the case here. Changing your ways is not easy. It is not easy to hear and it is not easy to do. It takes someone pretty tough to do what I am going to ask you to do."

Ed thought about this for a few seconds, and then I continued.

"I will always talk to you with respect, but I will tell you the truth, and the bottom-line here is that you are never going to reach your potential and you will never be truly happy unless you improve in these weak areas. You need to keep your strengths where they are, but you need to really train and develop these weaknesses." Ed just stared at his scores.

"If you decide to leave, that's your choice. However, wherever you go, you will always take yourself with you. In a year or two, your new employer will see these flaws as well, and you will be right back in this same place. That has been the cycle of your career," I told him.

Much to his credit, Ed thought about it for a few days, then decided to "give it a shot," to put it in his words. Unfortunately, while Ed was superior in his assertiveness, independence, and problem-solving, he was weak. He wasn't tough enough to face the truth and attack his weaknesses. Instead, Ed continued rationalizing his problems away and blaming everyone else for his shortcomings. I recommended to his employer that we stop coaching him. It was a waste of time and money. Ed was later terminated.

I also learned that Ed was on his third marriage and was separated from his current wife. All in all, it was a very sad yet common situation. Someone who is a bad communicator at work, is probably a bad communicator in their personal life.

Remember: Everywhere you go, you take yourself with you.

SALLY

Next, you will see the EQ scores of Sally, a director of tax for a certified public accounting (CPA) firm. You will notice that this assessment looks very different from the previous one. The first type of assessment is the colorized and most recent version of MHS's EQ assessments, the EQ-i 2.0®, which is the current version that I use with my clients. However, you will see that Sally's EQ assessment is a black and white version, which is because it is an older version, the EQ-i 1.0®. I have included it in this book because it shows you the improvements Sally made in her desire to become an emotional adult. It is one of the very few times where I was allowed to do an EQ assessment and Post-EQ assessment. I believe these results are very telling of what someone can accomplish if they put their mind to it. Sally was a lot tougher than Ed.

As you can see, she had many excellent scores. Her assertiveness and independence scores were remarkable. Her empathy, stress tolerance, and adaptability scores were all high. These scores made sense because Sally was a very assertive CPA, which showed up in her EQ assessment. She had been promoted several times throughout the years, but that was because of her great technical skills. Of course, because of these promotions, she was now supervising other people.

In Sally's case, even though she had great assertiveness, independence, empathy, stress tolerance, and overall adaptability scores, her interpersonal relationships, impulse control, and self-actualization scores were all 20 to 30 points below her high scores. Her assertiveness score of 134 was so high that it became the greatest detriment to her career and personal life because her other scores were so much lower. She did not have other strong interpersonal skills that could balance out her great assertiveness. This is a perfect example of how a weakness is nothing but a strength overplayed. Assertiveness is a very good thing, but not if you cannot control it.

Even though Sally's high level of assertiveness was a great asset to her as a CPA, it was killing her as a supervisor. She now had to interact with people and help them in their duties. She was unable to do this effectively because her aggressiveness was not tempered by her interpersonal skills. Subordinates described her as being "very difficult" to work with, "too demanding," "egotistical," and "very unapproachable."

SALLY'S EQ-i 1.0 ASSESSMENT

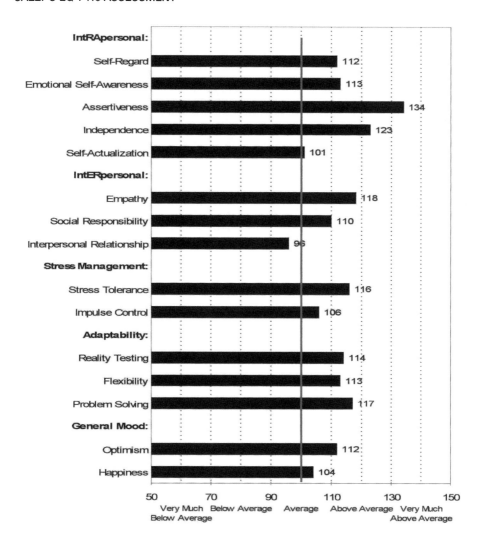

Trust in her department was nonexistent.

First, her EI assessment allowed me to show her that the problem was not with everyone else. It was with her. She was the one who needed to change, which is no small feat in and of itself. Next, her EQ assessment allowed me to target the specific areas in which she needed to improve rather than just telling her to "do better." I then gave her two or three specific strategies to develop her interpersonal skills.

You can't just tell someone to "grow up" or to "just control your emotions." The reason we conduct emotional intelligence assessments is so we can specifically target what the person needs to do to improve and increase their EI.

It is important to note that while developing Sally's emotional intelligence, we wanted all of her various scores to be as close to one another as possible in order for them to balance out. However, this does not mean that Sally should lower any of her current scores. Sally had excellent high scores, but the problem is that they were not evened out with her lower scores. The best course of action in helping Sally is then to help her bring her lower scores up.

I told Sally that she needed to create an environment where it was safe to speak up. She needed to get her employees to trust her, which meant not attacking them whenever they disagreed with her. That was her standard operating procedure, and everyone knew it. We worked on her self-control by looking at what makes humans tick. She needed to slow down and control herself. She understood how emotionally charged humans are and why her reactions were killing her career.

"So," she asked. "I should just assume everyone is an emotional child?"

"Yes," I told her. "If they end up being emotionally mature, you've caught a break. But the way you are reacting now whenever anyone disagrees with you is proving to your people that it is not safe to discuss anything with you and disagree with your opinion."

We worked extensively on how Sally could better control herself and resolve conflict. After about nine months of working on these areas, her relationships improved greatly. Her opinions did not change, but she no longer came across as an egotist and was able to build some trust with many of her subordinates and peers. As a result, her job was no longer in jeopardy.

I then conducted a follow-up EQ test with Sally about a year later. In the first assessment, she scored very low because she reacted emotionally without thinking whenever she had a conflict with someone. However, she boosted her scores tremendously by simply taking an extra five or six seconds to actually engage her frontal lobes and using her Verbal Jeet Skills. As a result, she was able to sit back, listen, and then work to resolve whatever conflict was at hand. In the end, her employees had a newfound respect for her. She proved to them it was indeed safe to come see her and disagree.

SALLY'S FOLLOW-UP EQ-i 1.0 ASSESSMENT: ONE YEAR LATER

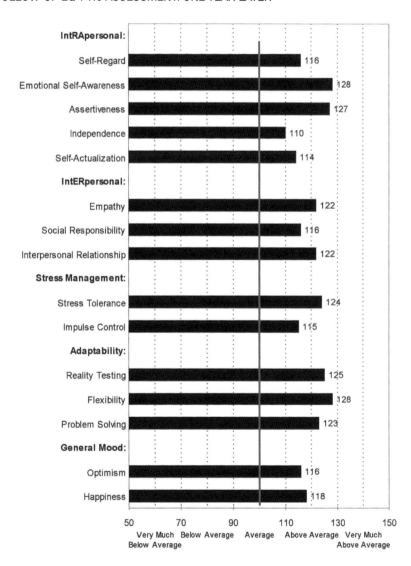

Sally's case is a typical one. As we move higher and higher in our careers, the degree to which we use our technical skills drops way off. Instead, our ability to build relationships, trust, and resolve conflict become much more critical.

BILL

Next, we have Bill. One of my clients was a social service agency that Bill worked for. He was their chief financial officer (CFO) and he had really ticked off the Board of Directors. Several of them wanted to fire him. At an earlier meeting, Bill felt that the board was not giving him what he felt was needed to accomplish his agenda. Bill blew up at the board because of this, telling them they didn't really care about the poor people of the city and they were only serving on the board to make themselves look good to the public and to pad their resumes. That, in anyone's book, is a really bad idea.

It was then that I got the call to go see Bill and have a chat. I tested his EI and saw some issues.

His sense of social responsibility was excellent, which made sense for someone who was the CFO of a social service agency. The organization's goal was to help people who are impoverished, and Bill fully believed in their philosophy. However, Bill's scores for his optimism, interpersonal relationships, empathy, and emotional expression skills were very low. In other words, Bill was playing the role of the martyr. In his mind, no one was as dedicated as him and no one cared as much about the poor as he did. In fact, that is what he told me in our meeting.

I looked at Bill and asked, "You used to have your own private CPA practice, didn't you?"

"Well, yes," Bill answered. "That is how I could afford to take the pay cut that came with this job. I wanted to give back to the community. I wanted to make a difference."

"Well, would you talk to one of your clients like that?" I asked.

"Of course not," Bill replied.

"Why not? Didn't you have some really stupid and selfish clients?" I asked.

Bill saw right away where I was going.

I then told him, "What makes you think that you can talk to the board one way, your coworkers another way, and the people you serve in yet another way? They are all the same skills and communication style. Customer service is nothing more than employee relations turned outward. Employee relations is nothing more than customer service turned inward. You cannot talk to the board differently than you would talk to a client. In fact, the board is your client."

BILL'S EQ-i 2.0 ASSESSMENT

He got it. We worked on a few techniques that could help him keep his emotions in check and focus his attention on his problem resolution skills. He apologized to the board, and to this day, Bill is still with the agency. Bill could take the pain and change his approach towards others.

I still use EQ assessments today to help coach people in how to improve, but I also started using the EQ assessment a few years ago as part of my interview process as a way to gain better insight into the candidates my clients were looking to hire. Because an EQ Assessment is a tool that only tells part of the story as to how a person will tend to react in various situations, I used it to help determine what questions to ask the person in order to get the rest of the picture.

Because I want to know how the candidate has handled themselves in past situations, I like to use behavioral questions. With behavioral questions, I will ask the person to think of a specific situation they experienced in the past, what actions they took in this situation, and what the result was. This line of questioning allows me to see how the person has reacted in previous situations, how their thought processes work, and how successful they have been in handling tough situations. When asking behavioral questions, I normally ask something along the lines of: "Think of a situation in which you had to lay off an employee. What actions did you take to do this and what was the final result?"

Of course, if the person says he has never been in that situation before, I would turn the question into a hypothetical question that puts the interviewee into a situation that they have not previously experienced. For instance, if the candidate had never laid anyone off before, I would change the questions to "Well, let's say you did have to lay off an employee due to budget cuts. How would you handle this?" Also, if they had scored low on interpersonal relationships, empathy, or impulse control, I would certainly want to ask that person something about how they resolve conflict. I would ask the person: "Tell me about a time when you had your plans at work changed by your supervisor, or a time when a coworker disrupted your agenda. What was your reaction and what was the result?"

As follow up questions, I always like to ask:

- "Is there anything you would do differently now?"
- "What if we called your former supervisor or coworkers and asked them about this instance? What would they tell us?"

I might ask the question, "Tell me about a time when you had a conflict with a subordinate. How did you handle the situation and what was the final result?"

Again, as follow-up questions, I always like to ask:

- "Is there anything you would do differently now?"
- "What if we called your former supervisor and asked them about this instance? What would they tell us?"

In order to see why someone maybe scored particularly well or poorly on their decision-making skills, I might ask the person: "We have all had an occasion where we were working on something that just fell through the cracks and didn't get done. Can you think of a time when this happened to you? How did you handle it and what was the result?"

Again, as follow-up questions, I always like to ask:

- "Is there anything you would do differently now?"
- "What if we called your former supervisor or coworkers and asked them about this instance? What would they tell us?"

If the person had never experienced this before, I would turn it into a hypothetical question and ask the person:

- "What would you do if I gave you a project that needed to be done in two days, but another manager gave you a different project that also needed to be done in two days? You are simply not able to get them both done, so what would you do?"

The bottom line is that I want to hire the best person I can for the company. I use these EQ assessments to gain some insight into their emotional intelligence, and then I flush out how they think with behavioral and hypothetical questions.

JAMES

The EQ Assessment tells just part of a person's story but it's an important part. A few years ago, I had a client who was interviewing James for a supervisory position. When I saw his EQ scores, I was blown away—they were fantastic. However, I still wanted to ask James various behavioral questions and see how he had responded in different types of situations. Based on his scores, I drafted interview questions that asked about how he delegated duties to his subordinates; went about resolving conflicts with his subordinates, coworkers, and his superiors; and how he delivered and prepared his performance appraisals. His answers were perfect, and I recommended that he be hired. James was hired for the position, and to no one's surprise, he was promoted within a year.

If you ever run across a James, hire him!

KAREN

I had a client who was interviewing Karen for a position. My client was an engineering firm. Karen was a young engineer who had graduated from a very prestigious engineering school. She had earned her professional engineer (PE) designation, which is the highest certification an engineer can obtain. She was brilliant.

The company wanted me to interview her to see what I thought. I had her take the EQ assessment to see where she stood on her level of emotional intelligence. I was more than a little concerned over her results. Several of her scores gave me pause, but I was especially concerned over her scores on interpersonal relationships, empathy, and stress management. I was also worried about how low she scored in problem-solving and reality testing.

When I met with Karen, she told me the only time she felt comfortable was when she was working on her projects as an engineer and that whenever she had to work with people, she hated her job. She felt most people were simply not as smart as her, which was probably true. The reason

JAMES'S EQ-i 2.0 ASSESSMENT

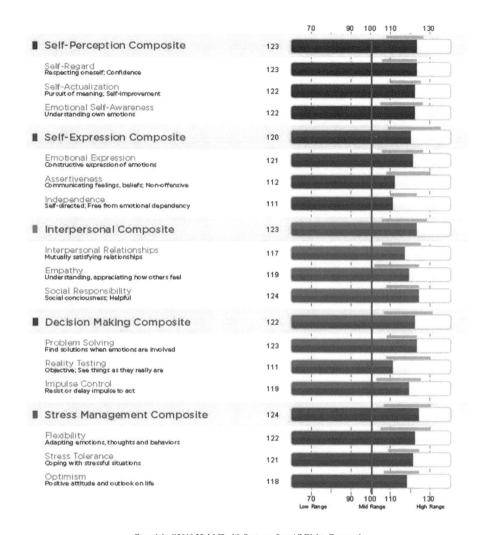

her problem–solving and reality testing were so low is because the EQ assessment focuses on dealing with other people and does not focus on technical skills. Whenever she was dealing with engineering issues, her problem-solving and reality testing would probably shoot through the roof. However, whenever she was dealing with other people, watch out. Her answers to my questions on relationship building, conflict resolution, and dealing with difficult coworkers were terrible. She felt that people should be dealt with like mathematical problems.

I advised the engineering firm to pass on her. If she was already an employee, then perhaps the company might want to invest in coaching

KAREN'S EQ-i 2.0 ASSESSMENT

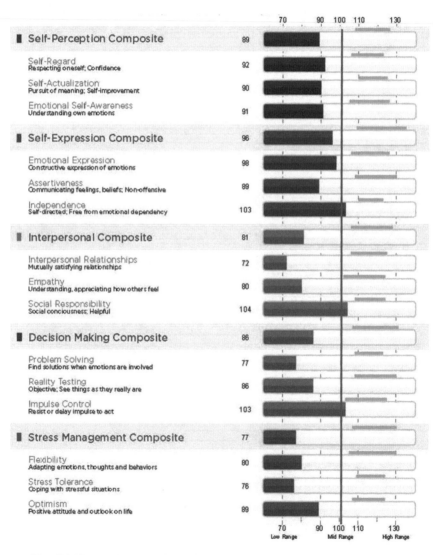

her, but as a job candidate, I did not advise it. I did not think she had the self-confidence and the strength to change.

Still, the company saw that they had a chance to hire a PE certified engineer, so they did. They also felt that she did not need the coaching I mentioned. Within one year, the company lost two other engineers because "no one could work with her." Karen was then fired. Shortly after that she filed a civil rights charge against the company based on sex discrimination. A large part of her case was based on inappropriate emails and comments that described her as not only being a "bitch," but also as being a "raging bitch," and a "PMS nightmare." (Can you imagine having to defend these comments in court?) Karen was clearly not the only emotional child in the organization. The company won at the hearing level, but due largely to these horrendous comments made in texts and emails, there was no settling this case or making it go away in a Position Statement. As a result, the total attorney's fees topped $100,000. They won, but their emotionally challenged managers and directors cost the company a small fortune.

The company also saw the light in stepping up its efforts in emotional intelligence training and testing.

Remember: nothing good ever happens with emotional children.

CONCLUSIONS

While your IQ remains pretty much the same throughout your adult life, your level of emotional intelligence is quite malleable and can be increased or decreased at any age. Increasing your level of emotional intelligence is easier for some people and harder for others, but most anyone can develop a high level of emotional intelligence if they can take the pain necessary to change.

CHAPTER 4

What Are Verbal Jeet "Kill Strikes"?

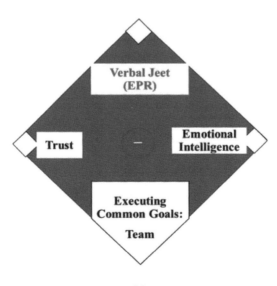

DEFINING VERBAL JEET: "THE VERBAL WAY"

I am always amazed whenever I present on emotional intelligence or Verbal Jeet and someone tells me that they are just not into this "soft, fuzzy kind of stuff." I will often respond, "Do you think martial arts is nice, fuzzy, feel-good stuff? How about boxing? Wrestling? Navy SEALS? When you find yourself in a street fight, you need self-control. Every punch you throw counts. They are called 'kill strikes.' In other words, whenever you find yourself in such a situation, you don't mess around."

Anyone who has ever studied martial arts immediately sees the need for emotional intelligence, or self-control. You will never master any form of martial arts if you cannot first control your mind. Controlling your body comes second. Mental toughness is a requirement. Anyone who has ever studied martial arts also knows the need for simplicity when they find themselves in a real fight. People don't go through their various katas when it comes time to defend themselves. Instead, they only use the kill strikes they really need. They need to think fast and use what works best. I don't think most people have ever thought of their everyday conflicts in that manner.

However, it is only a matter of time until you run into a conflict situation where the emotional stakes are very high and you will need to demonstrate a mastery of control over your ego and emotions.

"Jeet" in Chinese literally means "the way." Therefore, Verbal Jeet literally means "the verbal way." Verbal Jeet is comprised of three "kill" strikes: Empathic Listening, Parroting, and "Rewards" (EPR). These three moves are specifically designed to help you deal with these types of highly emotional and unpredictable conflict situations.

Chinese martial arts was, for hundreds of years, kept secret from Westerners. It was simply too valuable to share with the rest of the world. And then came Bruce Lee.

In the early 1960s, Lee established the Jun Fan Gung Fu Institute to teach an evolving form of martial arts. (Jun-fan was his real last name. Lee was his first name. No, Bruce is not a typical Chinese name.) In 1965, Lee entered into a martial arts match with Wong Jack Man. Even though Lee won the fight, he concluded that this fight had lasted too long and that he had failed to live up to his potential because he used the traditional techniques of martial arts. Lee concluded that traditional martial arts techniques were too rigid and formalistic to be used in the real-life chaos of street fighting. So, Lee further developed his own simplified fighting system that emphasized "practicality, flexibility, speed, and efficiency."

Lee's new system eliminated all the extraneous moves of traditional martial arts and only "kill strikes" remained. Whenever someone is in a fight, they don't need to remember anything but these because anything else just gets in the way of defending themselves. On July 9, 1967, Bruce Lee announced that he was calling this new simplified fighting style "Jeet Kune Do."

Unlike more traditional forms of martial arts, Jeet Kune Do is not rigidly designed with fixed or patterned moves. Jeet Kune Do is instead a philosophy with guiding thoughts and is designed to use minimal movements for maximum effectiveness and speed. Depending on the situation, the individual decides which particular moves they need to use at any given time in the conflict. I love Lee's concept here because it applies directly to so many self-help and conflict resolution styles professed by so many experts.

Unfortunately, so many of the communication programs out there are way too complicated for use in the real world of street fighting. You will often see someone profess the "7 Skills of Communication," or "The 9 Steps of Conflict Resolution" and so on. In the real world, however, conflict resolution does not follow a distinct pattern. It is not organized with formalized and predictable situations. Real world conflict resolution has a lot in common with street fighting. If you want to win in these unpredictable and highly emotional situations, you only need to use kill strikes. Anything else just gets in the way.

Just as Bruce Lee reasoned with Jeet Kune Do, everyday conflict resolution situations are messy and can often get out of control. When we are under fire, we cannot be expected to remember and use "The 9 Steps of Conflict Resolution." It is totally unrealistic. What we really need are simple and effective kill strikes.

EMPATHIC LISTENING, PARROTING, AND "REWARDS" (EPR)

The only three moves or "kill strikes" you will ever need to resolve a conflict are EPR. Of course, as is the case in any street fight, the exact order in which you will use these three moves is never set. Although we will often use them in order, that will not always be the case. Street fights, just like highly emotional conflicts, do not happen in an orderly fashion. With Verbal Jeet, however, you choose which of the three kill strikes you are going to use at any given time. Is it best to first use your E, your P, or your R? You have to decide, but then you only have to remember these three moves. That is it. Simple.

NEVER SAY "SOFT SKILLS"

If you are ever in a training class and the instructor tells you that he is going to cover "soft skills," run away. Think of it this way:

- If you cannot define something, how can you teach it?
- If you can't define it, how can you replicate it across an entire organization and change your culture?
- And if you can't define it, how can you measure it?

In any program, you must define your terms. If not, no one will ever really understand what you are talking about.

When I was studying communication at Ohio State, one of my instructors told us, "Words have so many meanings that they don't have any meaning." I remember thinking, "And I am paying how much for this?" What my instructor was telling us, however, was if you don't define your terms, what you meant to say is very likely not what everyone will hear. For instance, if I use the word "pound," what does that mean?

To different people, it has different meanings. A pound could be a measurement of weight, a form of currency, or it could be a verb meaning to injure somebody. Every word we use often has a different meaning to each person hearing it. It's important to define your terms in order to prevent different meanings from bouncing around in the heads of everyone in the organization. Real communication cannot happen if everyone is assigning a different meaning to what you are saying.

This is the exact problem we have whenever we tell someone to treat others with "respect." We use this term without first defining it. If I asked a room of 50 people what it means to treat others with respect, I would get 50 different definitions. Respect means something different to every person, and if I haven't defined my term, people will go with the first definition of respect that pops into their head. Far too many people try to be respectful in their communication but end up only dancing around the topic and sugarcoating their message. In the end, their main point becomes so diluted that the real message never gets delivered and the Sender comes across as being wishy-washy, weak, and incompetent.

Therefore, we need to define what we mean by the term respect, which is EPR. These three skills combined are what we use to show others respect. The logic for using our EPR moves is that it gives us a defined and easy-to-remember way to show respect for the other person's point of view in highly emotional conflict situations. Even though we might disagree with another person's opinion, we can still show the other person respect by listening to their point of view, understanding it, and trying to preserve their sense of self-esteem.

Remember: you are dealing with humans, the most emotional and fickle animal on the planet. If you recall from our earlier discussion, humans have an emotional system that will "kick" into gear at 17,000ths of a second. Humans can become emotionally hijacked before they even know what is happening, which is when the yelling starts and coffee cups go flying.

I have never met anyone who didn't like the idea of becoming a black belt communicator and gaining more control over their own lives. However, most people go about it all wrong. The most important life skills you will ever acquire are the abilities to control yourself so you can then address and resolve conflict. By becoming a Verbal Jeet black belt, which means mastering your EPR Skills (Empathic Listening, Parroting, and "Rewards"), which we will discuss later in this book, you can become a powerful individual.

CHAPTER 5

The Three Styles of Communication

RETREATERS, ATTACKERS, AND HONEST COMMUNICATORS

BUILDING A CHAMPIONSHIP TEAM

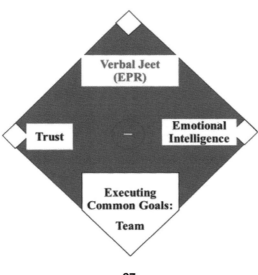

Receiver   **Sender**

Honest Respectful Communicators

ARE YOU A GOOD PITCHER?

Now that we understand what it means to be an emotionally intelligent person, it is time to use these skills and become an emotionally intelligent communicator. If you look at our diagram, the next step in our process is having the self-control to not be an Attacker (self-restraint), to not be a Retreater (having the courage to address important issues), and to use our Verbal Jeet (EPR) Skills to resolve conflict instead. This means we must first become honest people.

If you ask most people if they think they are good communicators, they will tell you, "Yes, of course I am a good communicator." If you then ask these same people if they think most people are good communicators, they usually respond, "No, most people are not good communicators."

Isn't that interesting? Most people are not good communicators, but I certainly am!

We hear such responses because when we enter into a conversation with another person, it is very clear in our heads what we want the other person to understand. We know what we want to say, so if the other person misunderstands the message, it must be that other person's fault. Why? "Because I told them!"

However, communicating with someone involves more than just telling them something. Everyone reading these materials knows lots of different words and could probably use them all correctly in sentences. Even primates have been known to develop signals they can use to convey what they want or how they feel about each other. That does not, however, make us good communicators. "Talking" is the mere physical act of speaking which most anyone can do, including gorillas. "Interpersonal communication," on the other hand, is a highly developed life skill.

Interpersonal communication occurs when we have a real dialogue with another person. A dialogue means that two people are actually talking with each other. That does not include trading emails back and forth with another person. It is not a lecture where one person talks and the other listens, like a monologue. It is two people actively engaging in an honest and respectful conversation with each other. I have had this discussion with several public speakers who naturally see themselves as great communicators. President Reagan was referred to as the "Great Communicator" simply because he was a phenomenal public speaker. However, being a great presenter does not mean the person is a great communicator on an interpersonal level. These are two distinctly different skill sets.

The art of interpersonal communication means you, as the Sender of the message, can get others to receive and understand your message so that it registers in their brains. It is having the ability to create a two-way street of mutual receptiveness, which means the Sender must take steps to try and ensure that the other person, the Receiver, will actually hear and process the message that they are sending in the first place. That is a dialogue. Granted, many times the breakdown in communication was indeed the fault of the Receiver and not the Sender. However, being a good communicator means the Sender of the message can "plow the field" for the seeds of understanding to take root for the Receiver.

Think of the Sender's responsibility in interpersonal communication like this: if you were a gardener, you would prepare the soil before planting your seeds. If you took the seeds and just threw them out into the yard, you would understand that a few would take root, but not nearly as many would grow as if you had actually taken the time to till the soil, fertilize, and then plant and water the seeds. Yes, that takes more time and effort, but that is the difference between getting a tremendous yield or just a few ears of corn popping up. Likewise, in order to effectively communicate your message with another person—especially in highly emotional situations—you must "prepare the field" for the other person to receive and retain the message.

The dynamics that go on between the Sender and Receiver with interpersonal communication are a lot like the relationship between the pitcher and catcher in baseball. You must have a pitcher (Sender) who can throw the ball over the plate and a catcher (Receiver) who can handle the ball when it comes in, even if the ball does not go exactly where it was supposed to go. It is the pitcher's job to get the ball over the plate, or at least pretty close to it. Unfortunately, too many times it is the Sender who sabotages the communication process from the very beginning by not creating a proper environment for the Receiver to actually hear the message that is being sent. A bad pitcher might throw the ball so far outside that the catcher has no chance of catching it. Those are the "Retreaters" of the world, because Retreaters will never be honest with you. They throw their message so far outside that the Receivers have no chance of catching it.

On the other hand, a bad pitcher might throw the ball at the batter's head, which usually starts a bench-clearing brawl. Those are the "Attackers" of the world. However, the real Senders, the best Cy Young Award pitchers, can get the ball right over the corners of the plate beautifully. Catchers love a great pitcher. These are the honest Senders of the world. All communication therefore starts with the Sender. A good communicator not only communicates their message clearly, but also creates an environment where the other person will be able to receive and understand the message.

The vast majority of people in the world today are really bad Senders and Receivers, which makes them poor communicators whenever they find themselves in conflict situations where the emotional stakes are high. (Remember the big guy at the car wash?) By far the most common problem for Senders as they try to communicate effectively lies in how they communicate. Obviously, these two styles of communication, which are clearly based on the fight-or-flight response, are the styles of cavemen. Humans usually pick our styles from between these two: retreating or attacking. However, there are three different styles of communication, not just two. These three styles of communication are: Retreaters (Flight), Attackers (Fight), and Honest and Respectful communicators. (Gee ... guess which one works.)

PITCHING STYLE #1: RETREATERS (FLIGHT)

A while back, I did business with a woman I will call Blanche. As negotiations advanced, I grew to know her quite well—she was a very nice elderly lady. After a few months of speaking with her, I concluded that she was one of the nicest, sweetest, most considerate, and most viperous, venomous, vicious people I had ever met.

Sounds contradictory, doesn't it? Well, actually, it is quite consistent. Let me explain.

To my face, she was as sweet and friendly as anyone I had ever met. But behind my back, watch out. Her claws would come out and she would attack the first chance she got. She would often smile and say one thing to my face, but as soon as I was gone, she would say something completely different to everyone else. Of course, she did not act this way to be mean to me. She did this to be "nice." She would often tell me that she "just wanted everyone to get along." In her mind this meant not telling me what she actually thought and slandering me as soon as I left. This is the very definition of a passive-aggressive style of conflict resolution. She was a classic Retreater.

Few people want to have conflict with others in high stakes situations, which are inherently highly emotional conflicts. Most people would rather avoid the conflict rather than deal with it. That is a basic fact of human nature. Still, I will often hear from Retreaters: "But I don't like conflict."

That is usually when I start laughing. Such a statement is like saying: "But I don't like the flu. But I don't like kidney stones. But I don't like diarrhea." Well, who in the heck does? The bottom line is that conflict occurs whenever two or more people disagree. It happens every minute of every day. As you are reading these materials right now, you are probably having some sort of conflict going on in your personal or professional life. Conflict is going to happen. It is unavoidable and you have no control over it.

What you do have control over is how you handle that conflict. You have three choices. You can:

- Suppress it (flight), in which you become an enabler and actually encourage the conflict to get worse by your tacit approval
- Escalate it (fight) or
- Resolve it

Those are your choices. Whether you have conflict is not your choice: you will have it. How you choose to handle it is the only decision you get to make.

Still, most people simply want to "get along" with everyone else. Instead of communicating information that may be disturbing, which could potentially expose the real conflict at hand, most people simply bury the information and ignore the issue. As a result, the person who needs to hear the information the most never does. Why would we ever do something so terribly cruel? Because we're nice people—and nice people stink! These are the "Angel Bullies" or "Angel Trolls" of the world. (Again, a "troll" is my term for a bully. Trolls are cute … but they are evil. I am trying to be generous here because, unfortunately, we humans are "hardwired" to be passive-aggressive, or trolls, or bullies. However, if you want relationships in your life, don't do that!) Everyone talks about how nice Aunt Bee from *The Andy Griffith Show* is because she takes care of Andy and Opie. She bakes pies. She always does something for her church and community. But whenever there is a problem, she does not address it. Instead, she sits with her friend Clara and talks about everyone else involved. She does not address the issue with the person involved, but instead talks about them behind their back. Aunt Bee was a Retreater. Just like the mythological beasts in Dante Alighieri's *Inferno* that occupy the Seventh Circle of Hell (Violence), Retreaters such as Aunt Bee create their own hell when they stab others in the back. In the end, their evil destroys their own relationships because, remembering Red's wisdom, Retreaters are dumbasses. It is Karma because they do it to themselves. Again, all communication theory is based on the most basic of human reactions: the fight-or-flight response. If given a choice in how to react when confronted with a threat, most people would choose flight rather than fight. Consequently, most humans are Retreaters. Therefore, most people that you know would rather avoid a conflict if at all possible. They are Retreaters.

Unfortunately, that means that most people are liars. They will lie through their teeth and tell you what you want to hear because these nice people follow the "Rules of Leadership," which are:

- Never upset anyone.
- Avoid all forms of conflict.
- Never address an issue. Ignore it. It will go away.

Of course, if you follow these rules, you will destroy every relationship you have in your life. These are the "Rules of Enablers."

In business, it is incredibly easy to tell when someone is "retreating" and lying right to your face. In fact, you see this all the time. The Retreater's voice takes on a stoic (and maybe even condescending tone) when they say something like: "we have decided to go another direction," or "that does not fit into our current culture," or "this does not conform to our values as an organization," or some equally vague euphemistic corporate-speak like that. Whenever someone is delivering bad news to you and they speak to you using vague euphemistic phrases—beware! You are talking to a Retreater or a passive-aggressive person, and they are the worst kinds of communicators on the planet. In short, they are lying to you.

Retreaters don't want to tell you the truth, so when they speak to you in nondescriptive terms, they are trying to cover something up. If you want to know what they really think, you need to ask them, "What exactly does that mean? Can you be more specific? I am trying to understand what exactly that means." Of course, if you have an emotional child on the other side, this will most likely anger them because you are forcing them to admit what they are really thinking. Most Retreaters hate to be called out into the light. They love the safety of their lies and get upset when someone does not fall for their passive-aggressive tactics. Of course, if the other person gets upset because you actually want to hear the truth, then it is probably for the best that you do not enter into that relationship—nor should you continue with it. It is nearly impossible to have a good relationship with Retreaters, or passive-aggressive people, because they will smile and lie right to your face. You cannot resolve conflict with someone who continues to deny the truth. (This is why marriage counselors are so busy these days. Sadly, people are not honest in their relationships, so they have to hire a counselor to make then open up and be honest with one another.) I once had a client that always used vague phrases whenever they did not hire or fired someone. On one occasion, this client fired a young woman who was the worst-performing employee in the company. She was always late with her projects, so they always ran over budget with her, even though they gave her the simplest assignments they could. She could never do her work correctly, even after they trained and re-trained her several times. They terminated her because she consistently did not meet expectations. However, instead of telling her the truth when they fired her, they told her, "We've decided this was not a good match," and "We want to go in another direction." When the young woman asked for them to be more specific, my client said something along the lines of "We just don't believe your abilities fit into our culture."

Of course, the young woman thought my client was lying—because they were.

The woman then filed a civil rights charge, claiming race discrimination. It was at that point that they called me. When I asked my client why they only gave her such nondescript reasons for firing her, they told me they were trying to be "professional." Unfortunately, this is a guise most Retreaters hide behind. However, it is not at all professional to lie or be passive-aggressive. It is disrespectful and cowardly.

"But that's what our other lawyer told us to say!" my client protested.

"Well," I responded. "How did that work out for you?"

"What should we have said?" my client asked angrily.

"You should have been honest. You should have told her that there were several issues with her work. Even though you had trained her and re-trained her on these projects several times, you were still having a lot of problems with her performance. She was doing a poor job, so you had to let her go. You don't have to go into detail regarding each project, but you certainly should have let her know that the reason for her termination was based on all the issues you were having with her assignments. Otherwise, of course she is going to conclude that her termination was based on her protected class," I said.

"But our other lawyer said if we got too specific, she will sue us. They said that would tie our hands," my client responded.

"The one thing I can promise you is if you continue to retreat and avoid addressing the real issues with your people, and then give such vague euphemistic reasons when you fire them, you are going to have a lot more civil rights charges in your future. This young woman knew you were not being honest with her, so she concluded that you were covering up something illegal. Again, you don't have to rehash each and every failed project with her, but you certainly want her to know that her termination was directly related to her work," I replied.

Unfortunately, too many people think being "professional" means lying through your teeth. It is not, and this is why so many people file lawsuits against their employers. This is also a big reason why there are over 38,000 assaults in the American workplace every week. Using such euphemistic phrases, or in other words, lying, only tells everyone that you are passive-aggressive and a liar. You are telling them that you cannot be trusted because, well, you are passive-aggressive and a liar by running away from hard conversations. You are being a dreaded Retreater. Still, this is what some of the "nice" people of the world do whenever they find themselves in a conflict situation, so they tend to destroy their relationships in a few other ways too.

When you lie to avoid addressing a conflict on a high stakes, emotional issue, your gut will start to churn. Because you have strong feelings on this important issue, your body interprets your emotions as an "attack" and will start a flight-or-flight response, and your adrenal glands will release adrenaline into your system. The mere fact that your gut is still churning over this issue is your body's way of telling you to address this issue because it is important. Retreaters, however, dumb down their guts and ignore this advice, instead hoping that the issue will just go away. Of course, it does not. It causes your gut to continue to rumble. If you are a Retreater, you will eventually do one of a few things, if not all of them, and all options are equally bad.

First, you may vent about the issue to others, which is just a type of gossiping. You may try to relieve the angst in your gut by talking about your frustration to others and you might even solicit others to join your side.

Sweet-but-evil Blanche really thought she was being nice by not telling me the truth to my face and instead gossiping about me behind my back. However, she is a classic Retreater who reasons: "I would never say anything to your face, because I am a nice person. So, I will wait until you leave, and then I stab you in the back." (Insert evil smile here.) This is how we get so much vicious gossip in our lives and why so many of us work in jungle-type environments.

Again, that is a Retreater (passive-aggressive), and it is the absolute worst communication style anyone can adopt. It always reminds me of the old saying: "If you don't have anything nice to say about somebody, come sit next to me." In the end, it is impossible to resolve conflicts or have trusting relationships with Retreaters because you can never focus on or address the real issue in order to resolve it. They will lie to your face to avoid the conflict. They will also avoid you entirely in order to avoid the conflict. These are the people who take the passive-aggressive approach by not returning your phone calls or by ghosting you on emails you send.

It is amazing to me how many times I have discovered after the fact that I had been in a conflict with someone and didn't even know it. There is no way to resolve a conflict with someone if you didn't even know there was one. Retreaters are simply not honest, which makes them the worst kind of communicator.

Every time I teach this seminar or whenever someone has just read my materials, I will get some manager who tells me, "I liked your message, but I really cannot do this. I just can't confront someone like you say we should do." To that, I will always reply, "Great. I am sure you are a wonderful person which is why you got promoted. Which other job in the company do you think you would like to do, because you cannot supervise people if you cannot address and resolve conflict."

The Four Horsemen of The Apocalypse

If you do not address a brewing conflict, eventually, the tension in your gut will likely turn into one of the "Horsemen" in what Dr. John Gottman of The Gottman Institute refers to as "The Four Horsemen of the Apocalypse": criticism, contempt, defensiveness, and stonewalling.

According to Dr. Gottman, whenever you find yourself engaging in these types of activities, the end of the relationship is coming. Each of these Four Horsemen will grow stronger the longer the highly emotional issue is suppressed and not resolved until eventually divorce, termination, or the end of the relationship occurs.

If you are a Retreater, you are most likely a Retreater in every aspect of your life … and that will be bad for you.

The first Horseman Dr. Gottman refers to is criticism. Gottman points out that being "critical" is very different from offering a critique or voicing a complaint. When you have a specific issue that needs to be resolved, you want to be honest and address it in a positive manner using your Verbal Jeet Skills. However, being critical of someone is different. It involves hitting someone at their core in a personal way. When you are being critical of another other person in an attacking and personal way, you are really just trying to embarrass the other person rather than trying to improve the situation. Consider the following two contrasting examples:

- Complaint: "I was scared when you were running late and didn't call me. I thought we had agreed to let each other know when we were running late."
- Criticism: "*You* never think about how your behavior is affecting other people. I don't think you are that forgetful. *You* are selfish! *You* never think of others! *You* never think of me!"

See the difference? The complaint raises a legitimate issue that needs to be addressed. The criticism involves a personal attack and uses accusatory language (focusing on "you did this"), which will only help to kill the trust in the relationship. Unfortunately, such criticism will then lead to the next and far deadlier Horseman: contempt.

According to Gottman, contempt is the deadliest Horseman of all and is the number one killer of relationships. When contempt takes over our style of communication, we become mean and treat others with disrespect, which means we will openly mock them with sarcasm and ridicule, will name-call and mimic them, and use offensive body language like eye-rolling. The target of contempt feels degraded and worthless. For instance, consider the follow exchange:

"What do you mean your report is late? Oh, no—you've been busy! I am sure no one else here is busy. Maybe we should all just ignore deadlines!

I worked 14 hours a day for the last month! Maybe if you worked a full day once in a while you would get your work done too. What do you think, Larry? Huh? Hello, Larry. Earth to Larry. Are you in there?"

Now that is contempt, and it is intended to make the receiver of the message look like an idiot. In his research, Dr. Gottman found that contempt is fueled by long-simmering negative thoughts the Retreater has been harboring about the other person. The Retreater has avoided and masked the conflict for so long that the resentment towards the other person has reached a boiling point, which then comes to head in an all-out attack. In the end, the Retreater's pent-up anger manifests itself in the form of contempt for the other person—often without the other person even being aware of what the real conflict is all about. The Retreater uses contempt to attack the victim in order to make the Retreater feel superior.

Contempt is also the single greatest predictor of divorce, according to Dr. Gottman's work. But then, I am still a nice person because I kept quiet about all your shortcomings for so long, that I now have the right to vent my pent-up rage on you. (Insert evil smile here.)

The third horseman is defensiveness.

Now, we all get defensive. That is just being human. However, this Horseman is nearly always present when a relationship is on the rocks. When frustration in the Retreater grows, largely due to their desire to deal with the conflict in a passive-aggressive manner, the Retreater will then fish for reasons to attack the other person. Of course, adopting defensiveness as a communication style does not work, and instead only tells the other person that we don't take them seriously or that we are blowing them off. For instance:

Her: "Did you call Betty and Ralph to let them know that we're not coming tonight, like you said you would this morning?"
Him: "I was just too busy today. As a matter of fact, you know just how busy my schedule was. Why didn't you just do it?"

He not only responds defensively but turns the table and makes it her fault. In this example, the husband thinks it is perfectly fine to defend himself in this manner, but it certainly is not going to have the effect he was hoping to achieve. Instead, his wife gets upset because using a defensive communication style is really another way of blaming the other person. You can feel her gut tightening up as she goes into a fight-or-flight response. A nondefensive response from the husband would have been: "Oops, I forgot. I should have asked you this morning to do it because I knew my day would be packed. Let me call them right now."

Gottman's fourth Horseman is stonewalling. This occurs when all communication simply breaks down. One person just withdraws from the relationship and just stops interacting with the other. I call this the "Three-Year-Old Syndrome."

"I am not going to talk to you at all! I won't return your calls, I won't look at you, and I am just going to ignore you like you don't exist."

Whenever someone is stonewalling, I always picture a little three-year-old with their hands over their ears saying, "I can't hear you…I can't hear you…I can't hear you." People use stonewalling as a solution when the other Horsemen do not work. By this time, however, the relationship is pretty much dead. This is as bad as retreating can get.

In the business world, managers tend to refrain from delivering upsetting news to their problem employees. Therefore, the problem continues until the manager is ready to terminate the employee, which is the "Rubber Band Effect." The manager eventually wants to fire the person for some small reason that appears to come right out of the clear blue. The pattern is classic:

> "I don't say anything…I don't say anything…I don't say anything…and then one day I've had it and I throw a stapler at your head, but I am still a nice person because I put up with your behavior for so long that now I have the right to give you stitches!"

So, in the end, when venting about the person behind their back doesn't work to relieve the angst in our gut anymore, we will adopt the Four Horsemen approach. However, you are the one that looks foolish as you take cheap shots at the other person or become short, rude, and curt with that person in front of others. In the end, you are the one who comes across as being untrustworthy.

Retreaters are classic Machiavellians, which means they feel perfectly justified in stabbing everyone around them in the back because they are certain that their cause is just. For them, the end justifies the means. That is why many Retreaters feel they can often gossip about others behind their backs so they can get their "digs" in while "supporting the cause." The biggest problem with Retreaters (i.e., gossipers, those who are passive-aggressive, etc.) is that they destroy the trust in any relationship they are in, as well as the trust throughout an entire organization. They are not honest. They pretend to be nice, but they are really just being passive-aggressive behind your back. It is not safe.

Actually, there are very few honest people in most organizations because humans run them. Unfortunately, many Retreaters have no idea the degree of harm they are causing. Instead, they truly believe that they are really being nice. It does not take long, however, before people realize that the Retreaters are talking about them behind their backs, which ends up undermining organizational trust. For instance, let's say three of us get together and start gossiping about you behind your back. When I say "gossiping," I mean that we are going to say some pretty demeaning things about you when you are not around. Of course, we aren't gossiping about you behind your back because we are mean. We do it because we are "nice" and would never dream of saying anything unpleasant about you to your face. We wait until after you leave to do this. (Insert evil smile here.)

Of course, after we are done saying these nasty things about you, what are the chances that you will figure out what we have been doing?

Probably around 100 percent. But how would you know?

First of all, you will most likely be able to read it in our nonverbal cues. Ninety-three percent of the messages we send are nonverbal, and humans inadvertently communicate the messages they least want to send because of how fast our amygdala picks up on these nonverbal clues. You as the Receiver will most likely get a gut feeling that something is wrong when you see us lie to your face. You will see it in our eyes, our lips, and in many of our nonverbal social cues. After you have thought over it in your head for a while, it will dawn on you what happened and why your gut started churning when you saw the gossipers: you were picking up on their non-verbal cues and they did not match the verbal message that was being sent.

Even if you don't read this deception in our nonverbal cues, someone will surely blab to someone outside of that particular social group. We all belong to multiple social groups, and as a result one of us, if not all of us, will spread our gossip to our other social groups when we get together with them again. As a result, the gossip becomes widespread and will eventually work its way back to you. Once you have discovered what we have been saying about you behind your back, do you trust us?

No, of course not. We have just proven that you cannot trust us.

No one believes anything we say. Instead, they watch what we do. If you tell people they can trust you, and then go around stabbing them in the back, they will think you are untrustworthy because you are not trustworthy. Retreaters are, by nature, not honest. And what about the original pack of gossipers? "Well, I would never talk about any of you … at least while you are still standing here. I will wait until you leave." What happens to the trust between the original gossipers themselves? It is also shot. It is not even safe to talk to your co-conspirators.

In the end, the gossipers destroy any degree of trust that might have previously existed in the organization or in any relationship. Retreaters create "jungle environments" that are devoid of trust. When you come into work, you feel like you have to put your back against the wall and shimmy down the hall so no one will "stab" you in the back. In the end, you can't trust anyone. Again, "trust" means it is "safe." With this type of atmosphere, it will simply not be "safe" to talk to anyone in your organization. As a result, you spend all your time at work on edge waiting for someone to stab you in the back and you are constantly on the defensive. We really need to take a new look at what it means to be "nice." These Angel Retreaters are killing us by destroying the trust in any organization.

I recall seeing a TV video clip several years ago in which a reporter compared the helpfulness of people in Atlanta and New York City. As a test, the reporter first walked around an Atlanta-area mall with a piece of toilet paper stuck to her shoe and measured how much time it took for someone to bring the problem to her attention. She then repeated the experiment in Manhattan.

Well … who do you think was more willing to say something? Was it the average New Yorker or the average person in Atlanta?

In Atlanta, it took several minutes for someone to come up to the reporter and tell her she had toilet paper on her shoe, but in New York, it took usually less than a minute or two.

Why did it take so much longer in Atlanta? What about "Southern hospitality"? Aren't Southerners supposed to be nice people?

Well … yes, most of them are very nice people. They are wonderfully nice people. Actually, on average, they are so nice that they would never want to embarrass you. So, they retreat and just let you walk around the mall with toilet paper on your shoe.

Interestingly, the camera crew recorded some people in Atlanta talking about the reporter as she walked by. Others were shown trying to run up behind the reporter and step on the toilet paper to pull it off her shoe without having to say anything to her.

So, who really did the reporter a favor? It was the "rude" New Yorkers.

Again, most people do not retreat to be mean, although some do. They usually don't have bad intentions at all. Most people are Retreaters because they are "nice." In reality, they just don't want to face any conflict in any form, even if it is constructive.

The Retreater style of communication also explains why so many marriages in this country fail. When I present these materials to marriage counselors I always hear the same thing from them:

"Yes! That is it! I see this all the time in my practice. The number one reason why people end up in marriage counseling or get divorced is because of retreating. People come into marriage counseling and pay $100.00 to $150.00 an hour to talk about things they should have been talking about at the kitchen table for the last five years!"

If you look at the divorce statistics in this country, you have to give their opinion even more credence. According to the law firm McKinley Irvin, the divorce rate in America for: [88]

- first marriages is 41 percent
- second marriages is 60 percent
- third marriages is 73 percent

Because going through a divorce is considered one of the most stressful experiences a human can endure, wouldn't you think that after you have gone through such a trauma once that your batting average would go up?

No. Because everywhere you go, you take yourself with you.

Of course, people get divorced for all kinds of reasons. Don't get me wrong. However, at some point, you have to stop and think, "What is the common denominator here?" The real problem with Retreaters is that they destroy the trust in any relationship. They prove to others that they are not honest and therefore cannot be trusted. When you retreat rather than engage in honest and respectful communication to address the conflict, you miss an opportunity to build trust. Because trust is established and built through honest and respectful conflict, people who avoid all forms of conflict thus fail to build any real trust with anyone.

Failing to address issues, or retreating, is the worst style of communication in which humans engage. Unfortunately, it is also the one we use most frequently in high stakes emotional conflicts, both at home and at work.

Of course, it is important to understand that not all conversations are important. I would estimate that 75 percent of the conversations we have with each other are pretty run-of-the-mill and nonthreatening. They simply don't matter that much. We talk about the weather, our favorite teams, the movies we have seen lately, etc. The emotional stakes are not very high in these situations and people tend not to get offended very easily. They are not highly emotional situations and are not critical to our overall relationships.

However, the remaining 25 percent of the conversations we have with one another really do matter. They define our relationships. They define the level of trust that exists between us. The consequences for each of the parties are higher because the issues involved are of greater importance than the typical discussions we usually have with one another. I call these conversations "High Stakes Poker" situations. Most of us lose our nerve when the emotional stakes get too high, and unfortunately it is when these High Stakes Poker conversations arise that we need to use our superior communication skills most. How we handle High Stakes Poker will define our relationships.

For instance, suppose I see that my wife has gotten a new hairstyle when I get home. Now, anyone who has been married for any period of time knows what to say when their wife asks them what they think of the new "do." What do they say? "Yep, looks great. Looks just great." Why? Because I don't care. I mean, if she likes it … I like it.

For the sake of discussion, let's say that I cannot stand her hair style and it is really bothering me. I tell her to her face that it looks great, but later turn to my sons and ask "What was she thinking? Did she let you boys cut it with the hedge trimmers? It looks awful!" I am stabbing my wife in the back by talking to our sons about the problem instead of her simply because I am too "nice" to say anything to her directly.

Obviously, this is one of those High Stakes Poker conversations that really does matter to me. How do I know that? Because the new hair style keeps eating away at me in my gut, which means I am getting ready to go into fight-or-flight mode to the point that I now talk about it behind her back. I start to vent to my two sons, which makes me a Retreater. As a general rule: if it is important enough to say something behind your back, it is important enough to tell you to your face. My gut is telling me that I need to slow down, focus on my emotional intelligence and use my Verbal Jeet Skills because ignoring the situation will be bad for me. I will get the reputation of being a Retreater which will kill the trust in my relationships with others.

If I gossip about my wife behind her back, my dishonesty will begin to harm our relationship. Once she finds out about my comments, which she certainly will because neither one of my sons can keep a secret, she will begin to think that I am untrustworthy and that I will stab her in the back whenever she is not around because I am untrustworthy and did stab her in the back when she was not around. But exactly how critical are these highly emotional High Stakes Poker conversations to the survival of the relationship?

In studies conducted at the University of Washington, Dr. Gottman and his team of researchers have been able to predict with 90 percent accuracy whether a couple's relationship would end in divorce by simply watching the couple interact for only three minutes.[89]

In other studies, Dr. Gottman and his team were 93 percent accurate in predicting divorce by watching couples for only five minutes to see how often they repaired their disagreements. Gottman and his team's predictions held true a full fourteen years later.[90]

To make such accurate predictions, Gottman and his team needed to observe the right kind of conversation. They had to observe a situation where the emotional stakes were high for both parties and the conversation focused on a topic that really mattered to both people. How the couple handles these High Stakes Poker conversations determines the level of trust in the relationship and therefore the success of the relationship.

Gottman's research shows that it is irrelevant how often a couple disagrees with one another. Rather it was how the couple handled disagreements that mattered. Gottman says that engaging in honest and respectful conflict when issues arise is critical to building trust and strengthening any relationship. The key factor in determining whether the relationship will survive disagreements lies in how much effort both parties put into trying to resolve conflict while also respecting the other person's opinion. Gottman concluded that disagreeing with someone while also showing respect for that other person's right to have a differing point of view makes all the difference.

People will always disagree with one another. That's life. However, addressing serious disagreements when they arise rather than allowing them to fester is critical to preserving the relationship. Retreating on highly emotionally issues will kill any relationship. Far too many serious disagreements are based on long standing differences that have been left unresolved and were allowed to boil over. Further, Gottman makes it very clear that more relationships die by "ice" rather than "fire," which means that retreating is the death knell for any relationship.

Having a Retreating style of communication is the most popular among humans because of our quest to be "nice," while simultaneously being the cruelest of all. We really need to re-examine what it means to be nice. So, if you want to really screw up any relationship you are in, either at home or at work, become a Retreater.

Enabling Is Evil

It is also important to understand that Retreaters are also enablers. Failing to be truthful with another person only encourages their current behavior to continue by giving it tacit approval. In fact, wherever there is bullying, you will find Retreaters at work. We expect evil people to be evil. However, even though most Retreaters are fundamentally good people who would never think of doing you harm, they are the same ones who are responsible for most of the evil that takes place in the world.

Think of every scandal you can remember, such as with Jerry Sandusky and the Penn State University football program, and you will see a whole crowd of Retreaters who did nothing but enable the villain in some way, shape, or form. In 2002, Mike McQueary, the assistant defensive coordinator for the Penn State football team, caught Jerry Sandusky, the head defensive coordinator, molesting a little boy in the Penn State showers. McQueary reported what he saw to Joe Paterno, the head coach of the team, the next day.

However, it was not until November 2011 that the assault witnessed by McQueary broke in *The Patriot News* by Sara Ganim.[91] Sandusky was then indicted on 52 counts of child molestation nine years after McQueary first reported what he had witnessed.[92] On May 8, 2016, the Associated Press reported that Penn State had admitted that it paid out large settlements to Sandusky's sexual abuse victims on behalf of Jerry Sandusky going back as far as 1971. Think of all of the "nice" people who enabled forty years of abuse! All of the "nice" people of the world who didn't want to speak up and cause any trouble. This type of enabling behavior happens all the time to one degree or another. It is time to be honest and use our Verbal Jeet (EPR) Skills to speak up and make our own workplaces and lives better.

Bullying happens everywhere you go, yet the "nice" people, the Retreaters, do nothing. Bullies get away with what they do because of the Retreaters of the world. For example, I once was called in to coach a failing retirement home administrator. I met with the CEO and the head of HR and they had some horrific stories about how this administrator treated her employees. As a result, turnover, Family and Medical Leave Act (FMLA) claims, and absenteeism were all through the roof. While it was clear this administrator was a technical expert in the rules and regulations of running a retirement home, she was an emotional child and a bully. Her employees hated her. From my other clients in the field, the message was clear: "Don't go to work there! It is awful!" Interestingly, this organization had two other retirement homes in that area. The employees in those other locations would not transfer into the one run by this administrator. They called it the "Hotel Transylvania."

I then met with the VP of Operations because the administrator reported directly to her. She told me that the administrator came highly recommended by the state department of health. They told the VP that no one in the state knew more about the codes and regulations governing retirement homes.

"Yes," I said. "But can she manage people? That is a very different skill set. I am hearing that she cannot, and that she should have stayed as a technician. I am told that she never should have been put in charge of people."

"That is not true," the VP told me. "She is a wonderfully caring person. If an employee is having financial problems, she will give them money to help out. That is what she is like." Of course, none of this had anything to do with leading people. Being caring does not directly correlate to being a good manager. It can help, to be sure, but if you cannot resolve or address conflict, game over. You cannot supervise people, much less lead them.

I then gave this administrator an emotional intelligence assessment. The results were not good. She scored very low in emotional self-awareness and empathy in particular. As I coached her in how to improve in these areas, her improvement was drastic and immediate. She read everything I gave to her, she had all the right answers, and she did improve her relationships with her people. However, I always felt that she was placating me.

When I met with the CEO and the HR person later, I heard about her improvement. I told them that while I was really happy to hear that, she did not seem genuine to me. She was too quick to agree with everything I said. There was never any push-back on anything I told her, which bothered me. I told the CEO and HR manager that she might be merely faking it and waiting for enough time to pass so she can revert back into her old author-itarian, bullying ways. This is what many people do. They put on an act to make everyone think they have changed, but they really have not changed at all. Eventually, this act wears them down and the real person once again comes out. If her change was genuine, it will get easier and easier for her to maintain improved behavior. However, if she was just trying to placate us so we will leave her alone, the strain will be too much for her and she will eventually crack. Faking it all the time is too hard. Her gut will start to churn as she builds more and more resentment towards us for making her play this charade.

A few weeks passed, and I was told that things were going well and that the retirement home was going to hire a new assistant to help the administrator with the day-to-day paperwork. This would free up more of her time to get out and see her employees. I had a follow up meeting with the administrator, and I was interested to see how she had been doing since I had last seen her. When I got there, I sat down, smiled, and asked her how it had all been going over the last couple of weeks.

She seemed nervous and agitated, which surprised me because I was told it had been going really well. She then smiled a bit, looked down at her desk, and said, "Fine, fine, fine."

That was it. She just weakly smiled and glanced around the room. She did not elaborate.

"Okay," I said. "That is what I have been hearing, which is great. I hear you are building relationships and trust with your people, but you still need to get more time out of your office to go and see them. I understand the VP agreed to hire a new assistant for you to help with that."

Instantly, her eyes pierced right through me.

"Who told you that?" she shot back.

"The VP. She told me that you still needed to get some more time freed up, so she agreed to hire a new assistant for you, which I know is something you've been asking about for months," I replied.

"I don't know anything about that," she shot back at me.

Wow, something is really wrong here, I thought. "I don't know. I thought this would be a good thing because so much of your time is spent on pretty routine paperwork. I guess they thought this would help," I said.

The administrator got a glazed look over her eyes and stared at her desk.

"What's wrong?" I asked. "I thought this was good news."

She did not look up. She stared down at her desk and would not acknowledge me.

"Well," I said. "I think you need to talk to the VP. I think she just wants to give you some help."

Again, I got no response.

Finally, I told her, "Why don't you just collect your thoughts, then give the VP a call? I think you two need to talk so you can both be on the same page."

She then just nodded her head, and I excused myself and left. I went out into the lobby and tried to call the VP. I got her voicemail.

All of a sudden, I heard the sounds of crashing files and screaming coming from the administrator's office. I went back to her office, opened the door, and saw her going into a fit of rage. Tears were running down her cheeks, her face was beet red, and she was throwing anything she could get her hands on across the room.

"What are you doing?" I asked.

"Get out! Get out!" she yelled, as she threw a handful of files at me, scattering them throughout the room.

I closed the door and instantly ran to the onsite HR person's office. I told them what was happening, but the HR manager was not phased at all.

"Yeah, she goes nuts like that every so often," the HR person told me.

"You're kidding," I asked. "I mean, if I saw another employee act like that, I would call 911."

"No, we're used to it. We just let her go on like that and then she takes the rest of the day off," the HR person told me.

"Does the VP know about this?" I asked.

"Sure," she told me. "We all know about this."

When I reported this to the CEO, the CEO laughed and said, "You know, this is really funny." (I remember thinking, "I doubt it, but go on.")

"She thought we were hiring someone to replace her. When you told her that we were going to hire an assistant for her, she thought we were really hiring someone to replace her. It was all just a big misunderstanding."

"This is not a simple misunderstanding," I explained. "First of all, this tells you how absolutely paranoid this woman is. She thinks everyone is as devious as she is, which tells you how she thinks. That is not good. Secondly, that is not a normal reaction. She needs a full psychological assessment before she should ever be left alone with your employees again. I understand she does this type of Jekyll and Hyde thing every so often. That can't happen," I told the CEO.

The CEO's shoulders sunk. The CEO confided in me that she also dreads coming in to work and having to deal with this administrator. The CEO then told me that she dreamt said had won the lottery and the best thing about winning would be that she would not have to deal with this administrator any more. Life would be great.

This amazed me. Even the CEO's subconscious is telling her to get rid of this person.

I looked at the CEO and said, "You know, you are not the one who should be nervous here. You set the standards and if she does not meet them, she's fired. And think about it: if you, the CEO, hate dealing with her, what do you think it is like for the employees she manages, those who are directly tortured by her behavior? She doesn't hold any power over you, and your gut clenches at the thought of working with her. What do you think it is like for the employees to come to work every day when she really does hold a great deal of power over them?"

Later, I found out that the VP had been lying to the CEO the entire time. She had covered up employee complaints and gave inflated reports to the CEO regarding any progress the administrator had been making with her employees. While the administrator put on a good face for a while, she did not have the positive impact on the employees that the VP had led the CEO to believe. The administrator complained that I had threatened her with her job in our meeting. Because of this, the VP and the administrator did not want me back.

The CEO then fired me and let the administrator go back to her old ways.

Just like with the Penn State tragedy, the administrator is not the only bad person in this scenario. The VP and the CEO are just as bad, if not worse, with the CEO holding the majority of the blame. The CEO enabled bullying by allowing this horrendous behavior to continue even after it became clear that this administrator was not capable of changing and supervising anyone, much less an entire retirement center. That, my friends, is evil. Whether it is the CEO turning a blind eye or "nice" people at Penn State keeping quiet for 40 years, the message is clear: The worst kind of evil in the world comes from the Enablers, because without them, evil could not continue. We need to evolve and be honest when we see wrongdoing or we will never improve. I think that Dante's *Inferno* says it best:

"The hottest places in hell are reserved for those who, in times of great moral crisis, maintain their neutrality."

PITCHING STYLE #2: ATTACKERS (FIGHT)

At the other end of the spectrum from Retreaters, we have people who just love to "tell it like it is" and attack other people whenever they communicate important information. People who assume the role of "Attackers" feel that whenever they are right, they can tell it straight and offend whoever they want because they have the facts on their side.

America used to see this type of behavior every week on *American Idol*. I will often ask people who attend my classes, "Is Simon Cowell a good communicator?" Some of the attendees get a puzzled look on their faces. However, I will then invariably hear some say, "Oh, yes! He is a very good communicator. He tells it like it is! He is just being honest."

"Ah," I reply. "So, let me get this straight. As long as I am just being honest, I can deliver my message however I want. As long as I am just being honest, I have a right to attack and insult the other person? Right?"

The audience then thinks about this approach for a minute. I then explain to them the other kind of Sender of the message: the Attacker. The Attacker is someone who explodes and abuses others, and then defends their attack by saying, "Well, you just have to understand that I feel very strongly about this."

"Oh! I understand! As long as you feel very strongly about something, you have a right to communicate like an absolute animal." (Oh yeah, that will work out well.) In short, Attackers are little "Devil Trolls." These little devils honestly feel that as long as they are correct in what they are saying, they can deliver their message however they want.

However, using an Attack style of communication is almost as destructive as the Retreat Style. Yes, Attackers are being honest, which is better than the Angel Retreaters who rarely tell you the truth and prefer to stab you in the back later. Yet few people will receive and process what the Attacker is saying even though they are being honest. The message will simply not register because the Attacker has not "plowed the field" and prepared the Receiver to actually hear the message. Instead, the Attacker puts the Receiver on the defensive, and most of his seeds of communication hit rough and barren land and never take root. In the end, the message is lost.

Remember: just because you said it does not mean the Receiver received it.

With Attackers, it is all overkill. Being an Attacker is like trying to kill mosquitos with a shotgun. Yes, they will tell you about the issue, but you are not going to be happy with the results. The Receiver will not effectively process what the Attacker is saying because the Receiver's body shifted into fight-or-flight mode as soon as they were attacked. That is one reason why Attackers are terrible pitchers: they throw at the batter's head, which does nothing but really tick off Receivers and stifle their ability to accurately receive and process messages. When Attackers throw at the batter's head, they clearly will not get any cooperation from the Receiver. (*Remember:* humans usually find ways to get even.)

When humans feel like we are being attacked, our bodies react in very predictable ways. The traditional fight-or-flight response is engaged. The adrenaline and cortisol levels in our brains rise, which allows our amygdala to commandeer our brain, which, again, is an emotional hijacking. Our emotions, not our logic, take control. Because our body undergoes a fight-or-flight response, the blood in our body is automatically and instantly re-routed to our arms, legs, and lungs. As a result, our frontal lobes drain of blood and our ability to think logically almost disappears. This is an involuntary reaction that our bodies have in order to prepare us for battle. Going into fight-or-flight triggers automatic physical responses. Our heart rate hits about 145 beats per minute, and our bodies redirect more blood to our lungs and large skeletal muscles, resulting in less blood flowing to our frontal lobes. Why? Because we are going into fight-or-flight mode.

For instance, have you ever wondered why your palms begin to sweat when you get angry?

It is because your body is lubricating your hands so you can pick up a rock and kill the other person. This helps to explain why we have over 38,000 physical assaults in American workplaces every week and almost two murders each workday. *Remember:* humans are genetically predisposed to violence. That is what we are wired to do. Never forget that.

When humans feel like we are under attack, we do not really hear what is being said to us. Our emotions are hijacking our brains and our bodies, and we are physiologically preparing to either attack the other person or run away. Our fight-or-flight response destroys communication—all because the Sender was a very poor pitcher. Attackers can never have a real dialogue with another person because the other person is way too busy getting ready to either attack or run away. This means that you cannot be a good pitcher and throw at the batter's head, but this is what Attackers do all the time.

I love to coach Attackers. Whenever I get an Attacker, I will usually say something like: "Okay, let me get this straight. As long as I am just being honest, and I am correct in what I am saying, I can deliver my message however I want, right?"

The other person will think for a minute and say, "Yeah. I know what I am talking about and I am being honest with them."

"Okay," I say. "Why don't we go to lunch? I'll buy. But because I am paying, I get to place your order and I am a 'tell it like it is' kind of guy, too. I am going to look into that speaker, give them your order, and then shout, 'Hey! I don't want any of you morons in there spitting on my food, either!'"

What do you think they'll do? But you were just being honest. You told them the truth. You told them straight. I mean, you really didn't want anyone spitting on your food. Still, many people simply attack others when they communicate and they feel perfectly justified in doing so because either they are just "telling it like it is" or they "feel very strongly" about this issue. People who say that are confusing the act of merely talking with interpersonal communication. Again, just because you said it does not mean the Receiver heard and processed it.

This is why most people cannot discuss issues related to politics and religion: they are emotional children. They cannot control their egos and emotions long enough to allow anyone else to have a differing opinion. Emotions run so high when discussing these topics that their frontal lobes run for cover and the amygdala commandeers their brain.

It never ceases to amaze me how many employers prohibit their employees from discussing politics and religion at work. The fear is, of course, that such discussions will only result in a lot of screaming and yelling, at best, or possibly an all-out brawl at the worst. However, if you think about it, this is the wrong solution.

We feel strongly about issues like abortion, gun control, immigration, and our religious beliefs, but discussing them (usually) won't instantly change your life or the lives of anyone else around you that very second. However, discussing difficult issues relating to one's job will affect most people immediately, that very second, and usually in a bad way. Issues such as being coached at work, getting a written warning, getting fired, demoted, laid off, or whatever else happens on the job are highly emotional issues with immediate impact.

Think of it this way: if you cannot discuss issues of politics and religion—issues that will not have an immediate impact on your daily life—what makes you think that we can have highly emotional discussions about your job, which are discussions that will affect your daily life immediately? You can't, which probably has a lot to do with why we have so many physical assaults in American workplaces every day, and why so many Americans say they hate their jobs.

That is exactly what Verbal Jeet is designed to do: give you the tools to *resolve* conflicts and not *escalate* them. Therefore, everyone in an organization needs to understand emotional intelligence and how to use Verbal Jeet, or EPR, to resolve conflicts. It should be adopted as part of your organization's culture.

Interestingly, most lawyers that I meet communicate like Attackers, which is how they can actually make everything worse for their clients. I always find it fascinating how we routinely turn to our lawyers for advice on how to handle our employee relations issues. Now, this is not a bad idea if that attorney has some kind of additional training in conflict resolution, communication, and emotional intelligence. However, this is rarely the case, and these courses are not typically taught in law school. In fact, the exact opposite is taught in most law classes. In law school you study the law … not communication skills.

When I was in law school, I was required to go to what I called "attack class." Of course, it was not really called attack class. Instead, it was called "trial advocacy" or "mock court." In these classes, I was taught how to "communicate." Or so my instructors thought. I will never forget my instructor telling us, "say it like a lawyer!" (This is code for "show your teeth and snarl.")

We were taught to be aggressive, act like little bulldogs, and to "tell it like it is!" The message was clear: you need to get in there and fight for your client!

Because my undergraduate degree was in organizational communication, I knew what I was being taught was wrong. I was being taught to be a classic Attacker—someone you would keep in the back room on a leash until you need them. I also knew that such an approach would do nothing but alienate the other side, stir the emotions of my opponent, and do nothing but make my opponent become less cooperative. I also knew that communicating like an Attacker would alienate those around me because they would see me as a bully, and rightfully so.

Unfortunately, today's society gives way too much credibility to lawyers. We rely on them to direct our employee relations, even though they have no training in this area at all. Unless an attorney has additional training beyond law school, we can often do a lot more harm to our relationships—and for our clients—than good.

In sum, Attackers are simply bad pitchers. They throw at the batter's head and really tick them off, and you don't want that. You want honest and civil communication, which cannot be achieved if the Sender is triggering the Receiver's fight-or-flight instincts.

PITCHING STYLE #3: HONEST AND RESPECTFUL COMMUNICATORS

Most people are poor communicators because they think there are only two choices available to them when they have a conflict situation: retreating (flight) or attacking (fight). However, there is a third style of communication that works to get you what you want and preserves the relationship. It is the Honest and Respectful communication style.

The only primary style of communication style that works is Honest and Respectful communication. This person is a "Cy Young Award Winner" (the award given to the best pitcher in baseball each year). This is the person who can put the ball right down the middle of the plate. As a Sender, they have great control over the ball. They never fail to get to the point, but they do not insult people (Attacker). They do not gossip about you behind your back on important, highly emotional, and High Stakes Poker issues (Retreaters).

However, to master this skill, one must first be an emotionally intelligent person, which means, at the bare minimum, the person must be able to control their ego and emotions (or amygdala) enough so that their logical brain (frontal lobes) remains in control. This means the Sender does not fall victim to the primitive fight-or-flight response. In other words, the secret to becoming an Honest and Respectful Communicator is self-control, self-control, and more self-control.

While there are many different skills one must master in order to supervise or lead other people, one stands head and shoulders about the rest: you must be able to address and resolve conflict.

In other words, if you cannot address and resolve conflict, then you cannot be in management, period.

Honesty: Seek Out and Resolve

So, what is "Honest and Respectful Communication?"

First, you tell the truth. Yes, I realize how simplistic that sounds. However, the vast majority of people you meet are not honest. They are Retreaters, which means they are passive-aggressive, gossipers, and enablers. They will smile to your face and tell you everything is fine before stabbing you in the back. *Remember:* I estimate that about 75 percent of our conversations with others simply do not matter. Therefore, we want to really focus our efforts on the remaining 25 percent—the High Stakes Poker situations when everyone's emotions tend to run high. These are the conversations that make or break our personal and professional relationships. It is critical for our own success in maintaining relationships that we focus on using our Honest and Respectful Communication skills in High Stakes Poker situations.

But then, how do you know when you are really involved in one of these High Stakes Poker situations? Your gut will tell you. Whenever you have a serious conflict with another person or "hard feelings" that keep eating away at you, your fight-or-flight response will kick into gear. As a result, your gut will churn and you will continue to seethe over the situation. This is a clear sign that this is no minor dispute for you and that you are not going to be able to let it roll off of your back.

This is why it is good to have a sounding board.

Sounding boards are people who will tell you the truth when you go to them for advice and whose opinion you trust. Good sounding boards will also tell you whether they think you are right or out of line and give you input into how they think you should approach the situation. You can even role play with this person and practice confronting whoever is the source of your angst. Because humans are unable to adequately and objectively advise themselves, sounding boards and mentors can be lifesavers.

Rather than sitting around and stewing on some perceived slight or talking about people behind their back, Honest and Respectful Communicators seek others out when they sense something is wrong. That is what emotionally intelligent people do: they seek the other person out and try to resolve the conflict because of the negative repercussions they will suffer if they do not at least try to resolve the issue. Seeking others out to resolve conflict is critical to maintaining positive relationships for many reasons.

Why Honesty? Fairness To You

In the previous section, we discussed how cruel it is to be a Retreater to the Receiver. Retreaters are enablers. The person who really needs to hear their message never hears it, which is how so many bullies get away with what they do. However, perhaps an even bigger reason why you want to be an Honest and Respectful Communicator in High Stakes Poker situations is because it is good for you.

Honesty: What Is In It For Me?

Reason #1: Your Health. First and most importantly, unresolved conflict causes your gut to chronically churn. This constant reminder from your stomach is a major health risk that is worse for you than smoking because you are constantly flooding your body with massive amounts of cortisol and adrenaline. In the end, this constant flooding of adrenaline and cortisol is:

• Aging you beyond your years
• Causing severe problems with your heart and circulatory system
• Burning out your short-term memory
• Causing you mental impairments

This is what people mean when they say, "distress kills." Therefore, seeking out the other person and resolving the conflict that is making your gut churn is vital to your health. Whenever you feel your gut continually in stress over some issue, that is your body telling you that this is not some insignificant issue that does not matter to you. You are going into fight-or-flight mode, and you need to start paying attention to that.

Reason #2: Impaired Judgment. When these unresolved conflicts arise and continue to percolate in your gut, they will change how you view the person you are having a conflict with and most likely give you a jaded perception of their motives. You will prime yourself to view everything this person does in a negative light, which will adversely affect your judgment.

Failing to have a clear and accurate perspective on this person because of these primed negative thoughts will cause you to make an error someday. You will eventually start to project your negativity about this person into your everyday speech. Others will see that you lack objectivity, which will harm your reputation. In the end, you will lose credibility because of your own impaired judgment.

Unfortunately, as is the case with most priming and projection situations, it is mostly subconscious. We will often fail to notice that we have lost our ability to remain objective, although everyone else around us will see it. This is all the more reason to have a sounding board or a mentor close by to see if you are being reasonable.

Reason #3: The Four Horsemen of The Apocalypse. As previously discussed, if you allow this churning to continue, it will build up. Eventually, you will fall victim to Dr. Gottman's Four Horsemen of the Apocalypse: criticism, contempt, defensiveness, and stonewalling. You will start venting to others about the people you are upset with behind their backs, which is Retreating. When your gossiping gets back to the person you're talking about—and it will get back to them—you will be labeled a passive-aggressive person and soon no one will trust you. You will become overly critical, speak to the person with contempt, become very defensive, and stonewall the other person by completely shutting down with the other person. Thus, these Four Horsemen have manifested in your behavior, and as a result, you will soon be viewed as being unreasonable, vindictive, or childish.

In the end, the people around you begin to wonder if you would make the same mean comments about them, which will harm your reputation and keep you from becoming the go-to person in your organization. You will be seen as untrustworthy and a backstabber. In short, your fear of addressing the situation will become a self-fulfilling prophecy—now you are seen as the "bad guy." Seeking others out and resolving conflict relieves the pressure building inside of you, which is not only good for your health, but for your reputation as an honest and trustworthy person as well.

Reason #4: Blurting And Exploding. If a conflict is left unresolved, the pressure continues to build to the point where one day we explode and attack because we can no longer stand the strain of the distress. We will then be seen by others as irrational, unstable, a bully, and maybe even a fool, all of which is just another nail in the coffin of your career. Therefore, it is important to seek out others when a conflict exists. Too many of us become upset with others for one reason or another, yet the person we are angry with has no idea we are upset. This is a "one-sided conflict," and one-sided conflicts typically go unresolved until the person who is feeling the angst addresses their problem with the other person.

When I was at Ohio State studying communications as an undergrad, we looked at how one-sided conflicts occur and how they destroy communication and relationships. I remember asking myself that if we know that these kinds of conflict exist, why would we engage in them and allow them to continue? Later, I saw that this is actually the most common type of conflict that we encounter and they prove to be terminal for every relationship that they touch.

CHAPTER 6

Kill Strike #1 = EPR: Empathic Listening

(LISTEN FROM *THE OTHER PERSON'S* PERSPECTIVE)

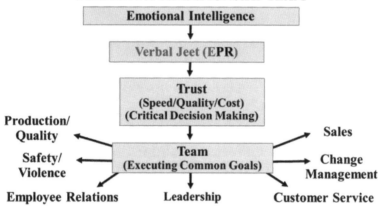

BUILDING A CHAMPIONSHIP TEAM

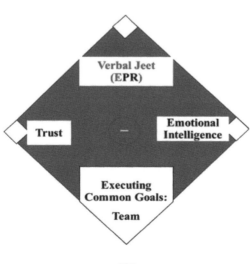

RESPECT: *SHUT UP AND LISTEN!*

If I have heard it once, I have heard it a thousand times: "Whenever I have to confront someone, I just don't know how to get started." Stephen Covey probably put it best when he said, "seek first to understand, then seek to be understood." In other words, "you need to stop talking and just listen!" The first key to becoming an Honest and Respectful Communicator means using a skill very few people will ever master: listening.

In most conflict situations, we think we have to explain our side so we can enlighten the other person. Of course, we do this with the best of intentions. We can see our own point of view so clearly that all we want to do is help the other person understand our side so the conflict will be over. Voila! Because of this, most of us start conflict situations by explaining our side first. Again, we have the best of intentions here. However, we usually do not listen to the other person's side of the story because we think it is probably wrong—before we've even heard it. The logic here is that, hey, if I can explain my side first, the others will understand where they are wrong, correct their perspective, and the issue will be over.

Unfortunately, handling conflicts in such a manner tells the other person one thing: "You don't care what I think." Of course, that is probably not the message you wanted to send. You believed the other person did not have all the facts straight or they were seeing things from the wrong perspective. You were trying to help. Unfortunately, as we all know, the road to hell is paved with the best of intentions. When we address a conflict in this manner, we are really treating that other person with disrespect because we are sending one clear message: we don't care what you think! Although that is not our intent, that is the message we are sending. In the other person's mind, if their opinion is not important, then they are not important to us.

Remember: humans are emotional animals, not logical ones. Our emotions—which includes our hypersensitive self-esteem—can kick into high gear and hijack our brains way before our frontal lobes even know what happened. When we feel we are being treated with disrespect, we react emotionally. In fact, when we feel we have been treated with great disrespect, we can turn violent in the blink of an eye. Humans want and demand to have our opinions heard. When that does not happen, like when someone cuts us off and does not let us explain our side, we have escalated the conflict into a dangerous situation that, at the bare minimum, will destroy any trust in the relationship.

This is one big reason why we have such lousy customer service these days: whenever I call a customer service line to get help, the representative rarely lets me explain my problem before they start giving me a solution. How can they give me a potential solution if they don't stop talking long enough to understand my problem? They can't.

Additionally, even if the customer service representative does let me start to explain, within 15 seconds or so, they will cut me off. It only adds to my frustration when the customer service person tries to solve my problem before they even know what it is! It takes us twice as long to get to the point, which only escalates the situation.

Listening is the most essential tool in resolving issues, and one that is a dying art. So, how do you get started in conflict situations?

First, as we already discussed, if you and I are having a high stakes conflict, I need to be honest with you. Something is really bothering me, which I know because my gut is churning. This is not just a minor irritation for me. It is a highly emotional conflict, so I must address and resolve it. If not, I will suffer all the consequences of being a Retreater. For my own benefit, I need to seek you out and resolve this issue.

So, I go to your office and knock on the door. I ask you, "Do you have a minute?"

You say, "Sure, come on in."

I sit down and say: "Look. I know there is a problem. It has been bothering me so I wanted to touch base with you and hear your side. I want to understand where you are coming from because I want to resolve this and make sure that you and I are good …" and then I shut up. I want to focus on the story from your perspective. I have to put myself in your shoes and use my empathy skills. Otherwise, I will not be able to parrot anything back to you correctly later (the "P" we will learn in EPR).

That is how you initiate a conflict situation: you raise the issue—and then shut up! It is honest and it is respectful. You are not retreating and you are not attacking the other person. You want to work with the other person and resolve it. Other ways of initiating a conflict discussion include:

- "I just wanted to touch base with you because what you said in the meeting yesterday really bothered me. I want to hear your perspective because I want to see if I am missing something here."
- "What you said about how I handled the project really bothered me. I'd like to understand why you said that we botched it. I want to make sure that you and I are on the same page going forward."
- "I understand you are upset with me over this issue. I just want to hear your side and resolve all of this."

All of these instances are examples of how we can approach the other person we are upset with, or who is upset with us, and tell them that we want to not only resolve this issue, but to preserve the relationship. If someone gets angry with you over something like that, you are dealing with an emotional child and you need to rethink the relationship.

ACTIVE LISTENING V. EMPATHIC LISTENING

Most people don't think of listening as being a skill at all. Instead, most people think of listening as something that just happens and it requires little or no effort. However, that is not listening. That is the physical function of hearing at best. Listening is without a doubt the most important skill you can develop to build your social awareness.

However, listening to another person is a lot of work. To be a good listener, we have to manage our own behavior and stop doing everything else we are doing. We need to stop shuffling our papers and looking at our computers, and we especially need to put down our cell phones. We need to stop talking (and it's not easy!). We need to stop arguing with that person in our head. We need to stop predicting what the other person is going to say and formulating our response while they are still talking. We need to focus on that person and what that person is telling us.

Developing and using the skills necessary for empathic listening or active listening is not a natural act for most people because of the way we are wired.

To be a good listener, you have to really focus on what the other person is saying and then process all of this information. You must translate their message into a language and format you can understand so you can repeat everything back to the person to their satisfaction (parroting). Being a good listener requires a high degree of concentration and a concerted effort by the Receiver of the message to truly comprehend what the Sender is trying to communicate. To accomplish this task, Receivers must practice these skills by adopting effective listening techniques.

ACTIVE LISTENING SKILLS

Before we can develop our skills as an empathic listener, we need to master the skills of active listening, which are as follows:

1. Concentrate on the Sender's message.

    This means clearing our minds of other worries or concerns not related to the Sender's ideas and not fiddling with physical objects, like pens, pencils, or papers. Receivers must ignore any external distractions—for example, not taking a call in the middle of a meeting with the other person. That kind of rude behavior tells the other person that you are dealing with more important things than them right now. Don't verbally tell someone they are important to you and then physically demonstrate that you are concerned with other things. Good listeners have to want to listen, and that means concentrating only on the Sender's message.

2. Learn to speed up your point-of-contact to the Sender's message.

    Too often, Receivers do not really start listening to the Sender's message until after the Sender has already started talking. Because of this, the Receiver usually ends up missing the first part of the Sender's message. To prevent this, Receivers should listen to the Sender's first few words from the beginning instead of jumping into the conversation a minute or so after the Sender starts talking. In most conflict situations, the Sender is nervous and will usually provide critical points in the first few seconds of the conversation. The Receiver will miss these important points if they are not ready to focus and listen from the very beginning. Asking a Sender to slow down or repeat something they said is a good idea—people tend to get flustered and talk much faster when they're nervous and doing so shows the Sender that you are invested in what they're saying and want to make sure you heard it correctly. *Remember:* good listeners start listening as soon as the Sender starts talking.

3. Listen for the overall ideas and the intent of the Sender rather than concentrating too heavily on the individual words used in the message.

   Many people have a difficult time effectively expressing their ideas to others, especially in conflict situations. As a result, they often use words incorrectly or out of context and therefore misstate what they were trying to say. Instead of focusing on the specific words used, listen for the overall message or context of their statement. Never embarrass someone if they misstate themselves, which is very likely to happen. If you correct these minor mistakes, you will escalate the emotions of the situation by seemingly insulting that person's intelligence, which will be bad all around. *Remember:* humans are emotional animals who are motivated by their self-esteem. If you attack their self-esteem, you have just escalated the situation.

4. React to the ideas being conveyed by the Sender and not to the person transmitting the message.

   Receivers tend to react more to their own personal likes and dislikes of the Sender than to their message. People we don't like can have excellent points. Listen to the ideas being conveyed, not the fact that you dislike the Sender.

5. Don't mentally argue with the Sender.

   Let the speaker complete their idea before you finalize your conclusions. Receivers should listen now, analyze later.

6. Do not interrupt the Sender!

   More Receivers are guilty of violating this skill than all the others combined. Let the Sender convey their message. No one can talk and listen at the same time. Receivers must stop talking long enough to let the Sender get their idea across, which is extremely difficult for some people. If this is one of your weaknesses, then try literally biting your tongue inside your mouth in order to really focus on the Sender's message.

Of course, asking for a clarification when something the Sender said is not clear is different. When you ask for a clarification, or if you need to parrot something back to the Sender to ensure that you are really getting it, you are still focusing on the Sender's message. You are showing you want to understand the point they are trying to make.

Do not try to raise a defense before the Sender is finished or move onto another subject. In those situations, the Receiver needs to keep listening. The Receiver will get their chance when the Sender is done. If that is too hard to do, this is where the Receiver needs to practice biting their tongue.

7. Take notes only on the important points being conveyed.

   Trying to write everything down will cause the Receiver to fall behind the Sender. On the other extreme, however, not taking any notes is just as bad because the Receiver will probably only remember a few of the Sender's important points. Therefore, Receivers should take enough notes as deemed necessary to properly recall the Sender's message. Again, parroting will allow the Receiver to see if they really got it.

8. Interject "encouragers."

   Giving the Receiver encouragers such as an occasional "yes," "I see," "okay," or simply nodding in agreement demonstrates that you are receiving the message and that they should continue.

9. Ask questions if a point is unclear or possibly misunderstood.

   A lot of the time, Receivers are embarrassed to ask a Sender to repeat themselves if they are confused, or if parts of the message are conflicting. However, if a Receiver does not completely understand a Sender's message, the Receiver should ask for clarification before serious mistakes are made because of the misunderstanding. The sooner misunderstandings are cleared up, the less likely the Receiver will go too far down the wrong path.

EMPATHIC LISTENING SKILLS

Empathic listening includes all the skills of active listening but goes a step further. Empathic listening requires the Receiver to also listen from the Sender's point of view. Humans are typically bad at using this skill. We tend to listen to others from our own point of view because we believe that because it is our point of view, it is the correct one—which is patently false.

Think of it this way: if someone in their twenties is going to communicate with a 50-year-old, they are going to have to look at the situation from both their own point of view and the other person's point of view in order to fully understand where the other is coming from. Otherwise, they are not listening to each other and therefore cannot understand what the other person is saying. Again, empathy is a skill that must be practiced. It is one of the most critical skills in emotional intelligence and proper communication. Trying to be more empathetic means putting yourself in someone else's shoes and asking yourself what it's like to be:

- nearing retirement and afraid of losing your job?
- a minority?
- of a different religion than your own?
- not able-bodied?
- homeless?
- in a war zone?

Asking yourself these questions is intended to put you into someone else's shoes and develop your empathy for others. Empathy is a skill. It is not reflexive. The more you put yourself into someone else's shoes, the more you will develop empathy and the easier it will be for you to use these skills the next time you need them. Looking at a situation from someone else's perspective will eventually become second nature because you have rewired your brain to respond that way through practice.

Jane Elliott was a teacher who pioneered tolerance and empathy training. She taught her pupils what it was like to be discriminated against due to some feature they could not control by telling students to treat their classmates with brown eyes worse than those with blue, and later reversed the two. Her intent was to teach the students about the unfairness and randomness of discrimination. These children described their experiences with Ms. Elliott as "life changing."

These types of experiences make a huge difference in boosting our sense of empathy so we can better relate to others. Once we have mentally put ourselves into someone else's shoes for even just a little while, we remember the ridicule, fear, anger, shame, and other feelings that come with intolerance. Ms. Elliott was teaching her students about discrimination, but she was also teaching them how to become more empathetic and increase their level of emotional intelligence.

You may ask yourself, what is in this for me?

Well, if you cannot have empathy for someone else, then you will not be able to relate to others very well, which will spell the end of your personal relationships and your career. In other words, you want to build empathy for others because it is good for you in all aspects of your life! In short, you cannot be an Honest and Respectful Communicator if you are not an empathic listener. Period.

FOUR REASONS WHY EMPATHIC LISTENING IS A CRITICAL SKILL

1. Empathic listening burns off adrenaline.

Say you work in a retail store. A customer rushes up to you, terribly upset over a return she was trying to make with one of your employees. She is angry, and she intends to take it all out on you.

Now, you have a good explanation for why the return cannot be made the way the customer wants it done. Still, you have an emotional child throwing a temper tantrum right in front of you. If you try to explain why her return cannot be made while she is going off into a fit of rage, what do you think will happen?

From your perspective, you feel like you can resolve this issue with logic. If you could get this customer to see your perspective and get her to listen to the facts, everything would be fine. I mean, you are just trying to help her understand how she can get what she wants, right?

Wrong!

If you jump right in with your reasoning while your customer is in the middle of this fit, what do you think she will hear? Excuses, excuses, excuses! Your customer is most likely expecting you to try to wiggle out of any responsibility and as soon as you start providing an explanation without listening to her side first—bam! It all becomes a self-fulfilling prophesy. She knew you were going to do this! She knew you were not going to take any responsibility. You are going to try to weasel out of this situation or hide behind some store policy.

Think about it: you are trying to logically explain the facts of this situation to a very angry person. Your customer's brain is flooding with adrenaline and cortisol, so trying to explain yourself to her is probably going to enrage her even more. So, what can you say to someone who is this upset?

Nothing. There isn't anything you can say that is going to fix the situation. Instead, you need to let the person vent. You keep your cool and tell the person empathetic statements such as, "I see," or "I understand. I would be upset and frustrated, too." You are not agreeing with the person, but you are validating their point of view. (This is called a "Reward," which we will discuss in more detail later.) You are telling this person that you understand and can fully empathize with their situation and frustration. In other words, you listened to this person empathically.

Think about it: you could have the best and most logical explanation in the world, but anything that you say while someone's brain is flooding with adrenaline is going to sound like excuses. Instead, you empathize, listen, and give empathic rewards.

Yes, this is hard to do. However, as with our example, your customer cannot continue on with this tirade for long. It takes too much energy. As you remain in control, she might see how unreasonable she is being. Not enraging your customer further will allow her to burn off this adrenaline. You can always tell when an angry person has burned off their adrenaline because they hit the wall. They run out of energy. Their voice falters, their shoulders drop, and they look exhausted. After this happens, you can now talk to them logically. You can now parrot back to the customer what you just heard them say so she will know that you were listening and understand.

If she acknowledges that you understand, then you can give her a "Reward" before disagreeing with her.

"I understand why you are upset. I'd be upset too. I can take care of this for you, but we cannot take the return the way you want…"

You can then explain how you can possibly resolve her problem and why your hands might be tied in this situation. Therefore, whenever you find yourself in a conflict situation, you start with empathic listening in order to disarm someone who has been emotionally hijacked.

Of course, to make this work, you must be able to control your own ego and emotions, and you be able to see and value the other person's point of view. Doing this requires you to first have control over your own emotions and ego, which is emotional intelligence. If you are emotionally intelligent, you will have the self-control needed to engage in empathic listening. Just ask yourself: "How much do I want to contribute to my own misery?"

Remember: we are most interested in helping ourselves here. Therefore, it is not in your best interest to try to give a logical explanation to someone incredibly upset. Anyone who is flooding with adrenaline will not accurately process what you are saying to them and will most likely still find a way to blame you. In order to fix the situation, you have to let them speak and then respond.

2. Listening is respect.

We live in a world where we feel disrespected on a daily basis. Unfortunately, everyone is so busy trying to get their own agendas accomplished that we often don't take the time to concern ourselves with anyone else. To have someone actually take the time to listen to our concerns these days is a rarity. That is why most companies offer such lousy customer service: they want to rush through your problem and give you an answer fast so that they don't have to listen to what you are saying. However, failing to listen to another person's perspective tells that person you don't care what they think. It's disrespectful.

Therefore, asking someone to explain their perspective and giving "rewards" such as "I see," or "I understand" shows respect. You are listening to the other person, which shows that you are interested in hearing what they have to say. People don't get angry because you disagree with them but will likely become upset if you don't even care to listen at all to what they think.

3. You might learn something.

In my class I will often ask attendees how many are card players. Several hands usually go up. I will then ask them if they would be better card players if they knew what the other person was holding. I will usually get a laugh and hear them say, "Well, yeah, of course."

I will then ask them, "Then why wouldn't you want that same advantage in a conflict situation? When you ask another person to 'Tell me your side,' that is what you are really doing. You are saying, 'Show me your cards.'" That analogy tends to click with most people.

That is one of the best reasons for engaging in empathic listening. Great lawyers will do this when they are litigating a case. The first argument they will examine is actually the other side's in order to figure out how the other side is going to argue. They then ask questions like, "Do I have an answer for this argument?" "Can I give an adequate response to that position?" or "Do I need to re-evaluate my position here?"

Why would you not want to get all of the information you can get before you openly state what you think and maybe avoid looking foolish? When you listen to someone empathically before voicing your own opinion, you are learning how to best approach the issue and how to send a message they can really receive. Maybe you did not understand the situation correctly and you are actually the problem. Maybe the other person will give you information you were missing and you will be more enlightened.

Even if you do not learn anything new by listening to the other person, by trying to engage in empathic listening, you will be able to see how the other person is interpreting the situation. You will see the other person's point of view, which is at the core of being empathetic. Even if you disagree with that person's point of view, you will see how they are looking at things, which is critical to resolving conflict. Only after you have the facts on the table and understand how the other side is thinking can you ever hope to resolve the conflict. Remember, we humans are designed to react emotionally in

17,000ths of a second, which is great when a wild, hungry animal is attacking us, but not so great for critical decision-making. We all tend to form conclusions based on our emotions, so we make up our minds way before our logical brain ever kicks into gear. Slowing down and first asking about the other person's side will help us get additional information, make better decisions, and, if necessary, possibly change our initial reaction. Empathically listening to others is therefore essential to critical decision-making.

4. Everything is a human Rorschach.

There is an old saying: Whatever you say about others tells me a lot more about you than it does the other person. Why do you want to start a conflict situation by engaging in Empathic Listening? Because it will tell you how the other person thinks.

For example, if you show someone a Rorschach inkblot and that person says, "I see a Halloween mask," or "I see a dog's face," or "I see a smiling clown," that tells me how that person's mind works. That is a pretty normal person.

However, if that person says something like, "I see two nuclear missiles colliding in midair" then smiles, you know that person has issues. Empathic Listening will certainly give you additional information, but more importantly, it will help you understand how that other person thinks.

CHAPTER 7

Kill Strike #2 = E<u>P</u>R: Parroting

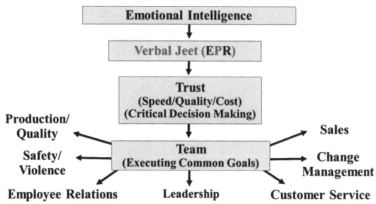

BUILDING A CHAMPIONSHIP TEAM

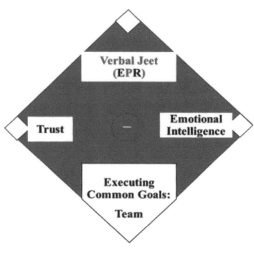

Once we have empathically listened to the other person's point of view, we need to "parrot" back to the other person what they just said. You do not move on in the conversation until the other person agrees that you truly do understand and have accurately processed what they said. Of course, you don't actually mimic back what the person said. That would be insulting. However, you do need to restate to the other person:

1. The facts of what they said so we fully understand their point of view
2. How they felt about what happened

You do not move on in the conversation until the other person agrees that you understand their point of view and how they felt about the situation. Engaging in parroting or restating someone's position and feelings back to them accurately forces us to engage in empathic listening. In other words, parroting keeps you honest as a real empathic listener. You can accomplish this by saying something like:

*   "Now, to make sure that I understand everything you just said, let me repeat it back to you. If I get it wrong, interrupt me and let me know"
*   "Okay. I think I heard and understood what you just said, but just to make sure, let me repeat it back to you and correct me if I get it wrong"
*   "I think I understand what you just said, but I want to make sure, so let me repeat it all back to you and if I get anything wrong, stop and correct me. Okay?"

It is amazing to me how often people can have an ongoing conflict yet neither side fully understands the other person's point of view. It happens all the time. Unfortunately, you see the opposite of this with our politicians. Politicians typically do not try to listen to what their opponents are saying. Instead, they take what the other side says and then try to twist its meaning into something entirely different from what their opposition meant to say. Of course, this is a big reason why little gets done in Washington. Whenever I am called in to mediate a conflict, the first thing I do is ask one side to explain to me the other side's point of view to their satisfaction. In over

30 years of mediating between two parties, guess how many times one side has been able to do that?

That's right: zero. It has never happened.

No one has ever been able to accurately describe to me the other side's position to the other side's satisfaction. If each side really understood where the other side was coming from, I wouldn't be there. This lack of common understanding is the death knell of resolving conflict. You cannot resolve an issue if you do not fully understand where the other person is coming from and what they want or need.

Empathic listening combined with parroting solves this problem.

In our society, many people score low on their EQ assessments in the area of empathy because it is not something we consciously value. Instead, we are taught to "be tough," "destroy other people," and to "fight our way to the top." It is drilled into us that it is better to be aggressive at the cost of being empathetic towards others. It is a "take no prisoners," John Wayne mentality. As a result, our EQ scores in empathy tend to be very low, and many relationships are harmed.

If you score low on empathy, chances are good your scores in interpersonal relationships will also be low because you are not able to see anyone else's point of view, which in turn will bring down your score in reality testing because you fail to see situations accurately and might misjudge something important. Because you do not have all the facts at your disposal to make good decisions, your critical decision-making skills will suffer as a result.

However, using your Verbal Jeet Skills (and in particular your empathic listening and parroting) will easily fix this problem. When you know that you are going to have to repeat back to another person what they just said to you to their satisfaction, you have to listen empathically. You are forced to focus on the message and understand what the other person is telling you. Parroting keeps your empathic listening honest. Whenever we disagree with someone, the other person's first assumption is usually that we did not understand what they said. In the other person's mind, he cannot believe that someone would actually disagree with his point of view. I mean, it is so clear and easy to understand in that other person's mind. The rationale is that if you disagree, you simply must have misunderstood the message. I mean, I have a rational and logical point of view here. "Surely, if you really understood what I was saying, you would agree with me." While this may be an ego problem, there is usually no bad intent here. It is just how we look at the world: we see everything through our own eyes. As a result, whenever we disagree with someone, you will hear them say something like, "No, you don't understand. Here, let me tell you again."

We humans tend to do this whenever someone disagrees with us. As a result, this restating of our various positions can go on indefinitely. Our conversation begins to look like a car stuck in the mud: We just keep rehashing "facts" and spinning our wheels in order to attain this epiphany of understanding.

Parroting ends this problem: if I can restate your opinion back to you, and you agree that I understand what you just told me, as well as how you felt about this situation, this constant restating and rephrasing of your position can be avoided when I later disagree with you. The issue of "you don't get it" or "you weren't listening to me" disappears. If you agreed that I understood what you are saying (parroting), and I disagree with you, then the issue cannot be that I don't understand. Instead, I just simply disagree with you. This is why we will not move on in the conversation until you agree that I fully understand your point of view and how you felt about the situation to your satisfaction. *Remember:* being understood is *respect.*

Another advantage of using empathic listening and parroting is that they force us to slow down and allow our logical brain to catch up and keep our emotional brain under control. When we slow down so that our logical brain actually has a chance to work, logical solutions become much more apparent and attaining a common understanding with the other person can happen.

It is also important to understand that in certain situations, you will also want to parrot back to someone not just what they said to you, but also how they felt about a situation. This is not important for all conflicts, but for some it is critical. Emotions can run so high that the others person's feelings should not be ignored. For instance, I have had adults sitting in front of me shaking with anger or crying from disappointment over what was happening to them. To ignore their feelings in this type of situation would be ridiculous. This is the perfect time to add a reward to your empathic listening, such as:

- "I understand you are upset. I would be, too."
- "I wish I could make this easier for you. I understand how upsetting this would be for anyone."

If we do not take the time in these situations to also acknowledge how the other person feels, we are telling that person that their feelings do not matter. That is a critical error in building and maintaining relationships and resolving the issue. I do not care what industry, profession, or country someone is from: humans are emotional animals who think once in a while. We are not thinking people who feel. It is not the way we are wired. Sometimes emotions can get so out of control that the logical solution becomes the least of your concerns.

I once had a manufacturing client where emotions were so out of control that fights were breaking out and employees were openly calling their managers "morons" and #!@!!$!. (You can fill that one in on your own.) They were also routinely sabotaging the machines. They would get fired for these acts of sabotage, of course, but the chaos did not end. When management tried to solve the problem by cracking down, everything just got worse. The root of the issue was that the managers, while doing their best to supervise and lead, were following the "Simon Cowell School of Management" style. Yelling at the employees until morale improved was all they knew. These supervisors really needed training in emotional intelligence and Verbal Jeet.

(By the way, all of these supervisors were living tragic personal lives. Sadly, it was all too predictable. Horrible EI and bad conflict resolution at work … horrible EI and bad conflict resolution at home. Sad to say, but this is a very common scenario.) When I told these managers that their employees were reacting the way they were because they were being treated with disrespect and believed we did not care about their feelings, the managers laughed. They told me the same thing most manufacturing managers tell me, "No, you don't understand. This is manufacturing. These guys don't care about their feelings."

My response is always the same: "Really. You think so?"

"Of course they don't," I will hear back. "All they care about is how much they're going to get paid and how long they have to work."

"Well," I explained. "I have worked in two different manufacturing facilities as a rank-and-file employee. I was one of those people on the line. That is how I paid for college. Actually, two of these facilities were unionized. I belonged to the United Steelworkers and the Glass Bottle Blowers. (The Glass Bottle Blowers union was with Owens Corning Fiberglass, or "Big Pink," in case you were wondering, "Who in the heck is that?") As you might know, they tend to not be very cuddly people. But I am here to tell you first hand: respect is everything!" I said.

"If you treat an employee with disrespect and do not acknowledge them as people on an equal plane with you, they will sabotage you."

Actually, I got a PhD in how to sabotage manufacturing equipment in these jobs. To this day, this skill has served me quite well in my current role as a consultant and employment/labor attorney. I explained further, "If you look at the unions' various websites, you will see one strong theme today that comes through loud and clear: respect. Workers will pay $600 a year to the union just to get treated with respect."

In this particular facility, emotions were through the roof largely because the employees were being treated like dirt. The only way to move forward was for management to admit its mistakes, parrot back to the employees what they were doing wrong, and that they understandably made the employees feel disrespected. We trained management and rank-and-file employees alike in emotional intelligence and Verbal Jeet in order to establish the best practices for having good working conditions and better private lives. Many managers and employees grasped these concepts and greatly improved while others did not. Unfortunately, those who did not adopt these concepts had to be let go. You can't build a team with emotional children.

Humans are not born lawyers, construction workers, dentists, and so on. We are all human, which means we are motivated by our egos and emotions. Failing to acknowledge and respect how someone feels about a situation when it is clearly important to them is an insult that will not go unnoticed, even if the person will not admit it. However, taking the time to parrot back the other person's recollection of the facts and their feelings will do a great deal to show that you respect the other person's perspective. Being respectful and acknowledging the situation as the other person sees it allows the issue to be resolved quicker and for communication to flow much more smoothly.

CHAPTER 8

Kill Strike #3 = EP<u>R</u>: "Rewards"

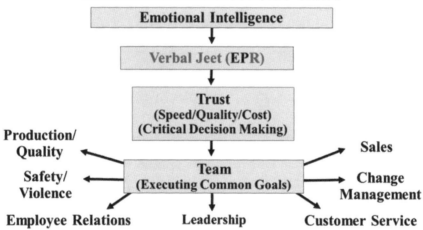

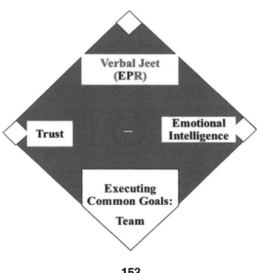

VALUES V. STUPID: MARRYING OUR OPINIONS

People disagree. That's life. If people feel like you have listened to and understood them, most will not get angry with you just because you disagree with their opinion. Even though you disagree with someone, you can still preserve that person's self-esteem by hearing them out, comprehending what they are saying, and "Rewarding" them when they disagree with you. I realize how elementary this all sounds, but in the famous words of Robert Fulghum, "all I really need to know I learned in kindergarten." Keeping things simple is often the best strategy.

Unfortunately, whenever we disagree with someone, we tend to interpret this disagreement as if the other person called us stupid. Of course, that is not what the other person meant to say, but that is what we hear.

When we disagree with someone—or when someone disagrees with us—it is more likely that our values differ from the other person's, not that they are stupid. For instance, in my seminars I will often ask the attendees if Republicans are stupid.

There is usually a pause and someone yells out, "They sure are!"

I will then ask if Democrats are stupid.

Again, there's usually a short pause, and then someone else shouts out, "Oh, yes!"

I will then say something like, "But that doesn't make any sense. The Republican National Committee has geniuses working for it. The Democratic National Committee also has geniuses working for it. How can geniuses be so far apart in how they think and what they believe?"

I usually get a long pause at this point (and a lot of blank stares) until I say, "Because their values and points of view differ."

Despite how quick we are to categorize those who disagree with us, intelligent people can disagree with one another without anyone being stupid. If someone opposes our ideas, it means they have a different perspective than we do and possibly a different set of values. Categorizing the other side as being "stupid" just because they disagree with us means that our uncontrolled ego is starting to control us. That is our issue, not theirs.

I saw this phenomenon alive and well in the 2008 presidential debates when Senator McCain disagreed with then-Senator Obama over whether the president of the United States should meet with the leaders of certain foreign countries without first setting preconditions. When it was Senator McCain's turn to speak, I found it interesting that he claimed they disagreed on this issue because Senator Obama did not understand.

Somehow, I doubt that was the case.

Not only did Barack Obama graduate *magna cum laude* from Harvard Law School, but he was also editor-in-chief and later president of the *Harvard Law Review*. To even be on the law review means you are in the top 10 percent to 20 percent of your class depending on which law school you attend. Regardless of whether he agreed with Senator McCain on certain issues, I am quite certain that Obama understood the situation. He simply disagreed with Senator McCain. That is the root of our problem. We think that anyone who disagrees with us simply does not understand what is going on or that they are stupid. Emotionally, it rarely dawns on us that intelligent and rational minds can have different value systems. Instead, we label the other person as being stupid.

I think of Henry Fonda and Jimmy Stewart when I discuss being mature enough to disagree with others. Fonda and Stewart were best friends for many years. However, Fonda was a very strong, liberal Democrat throughout his life and Stewart was a very conservative Republican. Still, they remained the best of friends. This can happen because emotionally intelligent people realize that their opinions can differ from others. The disagreement often has nothing to with intelligence. It has to do with their values, which also does not mean that one person's set of values is either better or worse than the other's. It simply means they are different. Emotionally intelligent people understand this and can disagree with others and not have it become a personal or "intelligence" issue. It simply means that two friends have different values when it comes to certain issues. Still, they respect each other's opinions. They do not insist that everyone should think like they do.

Unfortunately, far too many of us marry our opinions. Many of us will lie and make up "facts" just to avoid being proven wrong. In our minds, if our opinion is wrong, then we are wrong, which makes us not as good as someone else. This tendency is because our egos are out of control, and it happens all the time. If you marry your opinion, then you will most likely be very resistant to listening to differing opinions and will therefore be reluctant to change your mind if you are mistaken. Far too many of us will continue to make disastrous decisions rather than divorcing our erroneous opinion. We would rather go down with the ship than admit we were wrong and change our minds.

Someone who closes off their mind to new ideas can be rightfully classified as being "stupid" since they will not allow new ideas to take root. Evaluating and then using new information is the basis of "critical decision-making." Regardless of your intelligence, you will make a horrible decision one day if you do not stop and listen to the input of others who might know what they are talking about, much like General Custer's decision in 1876 to attack a group of Native Americans in Montana. (Really bad idea there.) Therefore, whenever we find ourselves in a high stakes and highly emotional conflict situation, we need to be honest and respectful with that person—which means we need to use our Verbal Jeet Skills. Disagreeing with another human being requires a great deal of tact and thoughtfulness. Therefore, using the "Rewards" portion of the EPR skill set is critical. I put "Rewards" in quotes because we are not talking about a physical reward, such as money. Instead, we are talking about something worth more than money—a psychological reward.

Unfortunately, whenever we disagree with someone, we typically insult them by throwing a "bomb" at them. We make it about the person—not about what they just said. For instance, when various people are in a meeting disagreeing with each other, it really does not help the situation to say things like:

- "Oh, my God! You are dumber than I thought you were."
- "That is a really ignorant point of view."
- "Where did you come up with that idea?"
- "I cannot believe what I am hearing here. Am I the only one who has both of his feet on the ground?"
- "All intelligent people agree with this."
- "You must not be able to understand this."
- "Maybe I am the only one here who really cares about this…"

Such comments are akin to spitting in someone's face and are just little bombs we throw at the other person's self-esteem. Attackers love to throw bombs at others in order to make themselves feel more important. It is classic bullying. Throwing bombs at people who disagree with you destroys the trust in the room. It proves to everyone that it is not safe to speak up and voice a contrary opinion. As a result, communication dies. Free-flowing ideas and brainstorming disappears. Groupthink and bootlickers rule the environment.

Whenever we throw these bombs at others, we are attacking the person— not the idea. We are stating that the other person is just not very smart. We are not focusing our disagreement on the other person's opinion, but rather focusing our attention on insulting the other person. That does nothing but entrench the other person in their opinions even more. In other words, we have just dangerously attacked that person's self-esteem.

Attackers commonly throw little bombs like these into the middle of meetings at those who disagree with them in order to gain an upper hand and show everyone who's boss. These comments are not designed to be respectful of other opinions in the room, but instead blow them up. As a result, such attacks do nothing but alienate the other people in the room who hold a contrary point of view. The unfortunate part is not that Attackers rely on this behavior to establish and maintain superiority, but that we do not push back against this kind of behavior.

Throwing these bombs at others will only put everyone else in the room on the defensive, which in turn initiates everyone's fight-or-flight response. As a result, our guts will tighten and our adrenal glands will begin to secrete adrenaline. This will then speed up our heart rates, which means our frontal lobes will begin to drain of blood and become flooded with cortisol. Next, our brain's logical and memory centers will begin to go numb as our resentment increases. In the end, those of us sitting in the room will not process very much of what you are trying to say because of the Attacker's behavior. Trust is destroyed because you have just proven to everyone that it is not safe to speak up and voice a contrary opinion. Anyone who disagrees with you will be attacked for doing so. This kills free-flowing ideas and any level of trust we are trying to create.

Consequently, you, the Sender, just lost the battle. In the end, what you say will not be what the Receivers hear.

Additionally, such tactics later blow up in the Attacker's face. The Attacker is quickly viewed as an unreasonable coworker who refuses to listen to any ideas that are not in line with their own. Others will then start to attack each other, because a defensive and distrustful work atmosphere has been created. The destructive atmosphere only escalates from there. The Attacker's behavior is not forgiven or forgotten by others. Interestingly, it is the Retreaters who will lie in wait to later get back at the Attacker. These kinds of relationships and actions are why so many of us work in these "jungle environments" today.

Research into the neurological reactions in the human brain has shown that whenever someone feels insulted and their self-esteem has been damaged, the reaction in their brain is the same as if they had just been kicked in the shin. When someone throws a verbal bomb at us, our gut tightens and our brain reacts with a very predictable fight-or-flight response, which signals our adrenal glands to begin secreting adrenaline in response to this attack. Neuroscientists refer to this phenomenon as "endangerment." In short, whenever we feel like we are in danger, regardless of whether it is an attack on our self-esteem or to our physical body, all our brain recognizes is that we are being ambushed. So, our brain begins to prepare our most vital systems for battle. Our brain does not recognize the difference between the two. Thus, throwing verbal bombs at someone is the same as slapping that person in the face—literally.

"REWARDS" = VALIDATING ANOTHER PERSON'S OPINION

People marry their opinions. So, disagreeing with someone without giving them a reward is an easy way to undermine relationships and make an enemy. Instead of flat-out disagreeing with someone and risk hurting their ego, we need to think of protecting the other person's value as a human being while at the same time addressing their take on the issue. Think of it like taking a scalpel and surgically separating the person's opinion from their personal value. You are going to appreciate them as a person but disagree with their opinion on the specific matter. We do this by giving the other person a reward. Rewarding someone else's opinion would involve saying something like:

- "I can see what Tom is saying, but I also think …"
- "I understand all of the other varying opinions in the room, but I also think …"
- "I agree with what Tom was saying earlier, but there may also be some other aspects we might want to consider …"
- "I appreciate what everyone is saying, but …"
- "I do not intend to offend you, because I respect your point of view, so …"
- "I can see both points of view here, but I think I need to voice my opinion as well …"
- "Obviously, many of us disagree with each other on this matter. That is okay. Intelligent people can disagree. But my opinion is …"

Giving someone a reward does not mean that you agree with that person's opinion or point of view. Quite the contrary. What it means is that you are validating that person's point of view. You are acknowledging that you understand why the other person said what they said, why they did what they did, or why they feel the way they do. However, it certainly does not mean that you are agreeing with the other person—only that you understand their position.

Of course, if you agree with a person's point of view, there is no need to give them a reward. You are agreeing with them. That is good enough because you are telling them that you think they are right. You only need to give a reward to someone you are preparing to disagree with because you are telling them that you do not think they are correct. If you don't offer them a reward, they will interpret your disagreement as you calling them stupid.

However, this is a very difficult concept for some people to accept. Whenever I am teaching a seminar on this topic, I will often have someone in the audience say something like, "But I don't understand why some people do what they do. I can't give a 'Reward' to some of the things my coworkers do by saying I understand it."

I will then reply, "You mean that you do not agree with the other person, right? I mean, you certainly have the capability to understand another person's point of view. That is empathy. You ensure that you have a common understanding with the other person when you parrot what they said back to them. If you cannot see someone else's point of view, regardless of whether you agree with them or not, then that means you are incapable of having empathy for anyone who thinks differently from you."

I will usually get a funny stare at this point or the person will say something like, "But how can you say that you understand some of the confusing and senseless things people do?"

To that, I will ask the audience, "Well, has anyone ever seen the television show, *Criminal Minds*?"

Several hands will usually go up.

I will then ask the audience, "So, do you all just like psychopathic killers?"

The audience will then usually chuckle a bit, so I ask them, "Well, if you're not into psycho-killers, why do you watch the show?"

I will then get an answer from someone that says, "I like to watch how the FBI figures out who is committing the murders."

"And how do they do that?" I will ask the person.

"They create a profile of the killer. They try to figure out why the killer is doing what he is doing and what motivates him," the person will say.

"And that is what we are trying to do here. The FBI does not agree with these killers and they certainly don't condone what these killers are doing. But in order to catch them, the FBI must understand why they're doing what they're doing. If you cannot get inside another person's head and figure out their motivations, then you will never understand anyone who thinks differently from you—and that will be bad for you. In other words, if the FBI can understand the mind of a psycho-killer, can't you figure out what makes an annoying coworker or customer tick?"

The premise of *Criminal Minds* is that people always do things for a reason. It might not be a good reason, but humans typically do not do things without a reason. Therefore, it is important to understand the neurology of people so we can better understand why they do what they do. If you can understand that, you will have a great advantage in resolving conflicts because you will better understand how to keep someone off the defensive. Whenever I hear someone trying to resolve a conflict and then say something like, "Well, you just don't know what you are talking about," I see a person who does not understand the human animal.

Validating another person's opinion is not agreement. It simply shows respect for a contrary point of view. Rewarding another person's right to have their own perspective separates their opinion from them, and thus preserves their self-esteem. Consequently, rewarding someone when we disagree with them should be something we do routinely. It should become a habit because it affords respect and helps to build trust, which means you are creating a safe environment where others can disagree with you.

If you recall, I stated earlier that in a street fight, you never really know which move will be the most appropriate to use. What move you need to use depends largely on what the other person does. You need to react to their move. A verbal conflict is a lot like a street fight in this way: you never know which move you will need to use first. Is it the "E," the "P," or the "R?"(By now, you should know what each of these letters means. If not, drink some coffee, or a 5-Hour energy, and start over.)

I have found that many times the most useful move to use is the "R," especially when I am dealing with people who need constant reassurance. Nevertheless, unless we have already established a very trusting relationship with the other person, we need to give everyone who disagrees with us "Rewards" every time we have a dispute. That is our best chance of gaining a common understanding with one another because it shows respect for that other person and protects their self-esteem.

Also, it is important to understand that giving someone a reward means rewarding their point of view on a particular issue, not giving that person a broad compliment. Such statements tend to only irritate and insult the person. It makes them feel as if they are being manipulated and patronized. For instance, when I was teaching these materials to a human resource group, one person was role-playing and practicing giving "Rewards" to an employee. They started their discussion with the employee by saying, "You know, Frank, you are a very valuable and trusted employee…"

At that point, I stopped the exercise to clarify what it means to give a reward to someone as opposed to giving them general compliments. Giving broad compliments to someone is not giving them a reward. Telling someone that they are "valuable" to the organization or giving them some other vague compliment like that sounds like you are simply trying to pacify that person instead of actively thinking about and considering their point of view on the situation. It does not really mean anything. It sounds patronizing and is therefore insulting. Instead, giving a reward to someone is very specific. Giving a "Reward" to someone means you are going to validate their point of view on this particular topic. You are not going to give the person a broad compliment. Instead, you are recognizing the validity of their point of view on this particular issue … period. A "Reward" is very specific and precise. The simple gesture of saying "I understand," and proving that you do actually understand—which you do because of your ability to parrot back what the other person told you—can make all the difference in resolving a conflict situation. It is simply showing respect.

CHAPTER 9

The Verbal Jeet Coaching Process

I honestly cannot get through a day without using my Verbal Jeet (EPR) Skills. Therefore, I thought a good way to wrap up this book would be to outline for you this entire process of conflict resolution and apply it to a real-world situation.

GAMES...

The various games people play with each other to avoid taking accountability for their actions are worth looking at in a little more detail. Too many people in this world fail to take accountability for their actions. I think this lack of accountability has grown to a national and worldwide epidemic and is at the core of many of our unresolved problems. Dr. Phil has fostered a very successful daytime self-help television show based upon this growing issue. Actually, watching *Dr. Phil* every so often is free training in account-ability. It is amazing to see his guests play all kinds of games with him so they can rationalize away their bad behavior and avoid being held accountable for their actions.

Do we play these games? Every day.

We study so hard to learn these various games for the first five or six years of our lives and then spend a lifetime perfecting them.

Most of these games take the following forms:

1. Deflection

Deflection occurs when an individual tries to blame you for their problems or their behavior instead of taking responsibility for their actions or behavior. We hear this when someone uses phrases such as:

- "It's not my fault! You yelled at me and made me mad."
- "You are harassing me! You are creating a Hostile Work Environment." (Sometimes this is true … and sometimes it is not. If there is not validity to the statement, then it could very likely be a game.)
- "You're just doing this because I _____ (belong to a protected class such as age, filed a Workers' Compensation claim, complained about management, and so on)." Again, sometimes this is true … and sometimes it is not. Again, if there is not validity to the statement, it could very likely be a game.
- "You're not fair!"
- "You don't listen to us!"
- "This place stinks—and management is filled with idiots!"

The strategy here is this: "if I can put you on the defensive, you will stop bothering me and lower your standards, which lets me off the hook."

2. Diversion (or "look over here")

Diversion occurs when an individual points to others who are also exhibiting poor behavior in order to distract from their own behaviors and actions. We hear this when someone uses phrases such as:

- "What about everyone else? Fred is doing this too!"
- "What about Betty? She is a lot worse than me!"
- "What about Frank? He started it!"

At this point, I typically feel like an exasperated parent and think to myself, "I will talk to your brother later. I am talking to you right now." The strategy here is this: "If I can get you to focus on someone else's behavior, you will stop looking at me and I will get off the hook."

3. Stonewalling

Stonewalling occurs when the individual simply denies your point of view. The person just disagrees and uses phrases such as:

- "Well, the company is wrong. It should not be done that way."
- "That's not my job. I don't have to do that."
- "I don't see it that way!"

The strategy here is this: "If I can just deny what you are saying, then maybe you will question the standard you are trying to enforce. I am hoping you will stop bothering me and lower the standard, which will let me off the hook."

4. Victim Mentality

Victim mentality occurs when the individual tries to play the martyr or victim. The person just simply falls on their own sword and says such things as:

- "Well, I will just work until I fall over to get it all done…"
- "I just won't talk to anyone anymore…"
- "You are all against me."
- "So, we should just tell the client that we can't do that…"

This is also called "malicious obedience." With malicious obedience, the person will literally do exactly what you told them to do and ignore all common sense just to make everything worse, like hanging up on a customer at precisely 5:00 p.m. because you told them not to work any overtime. Of course, this person is purposely trying to harm the organization or the relationship by undercutting your overall goals. The strategy here is this: "If I can take this situation to the absurd, I can play the victim and get you to lower the standard."

All these "games" are used to accomplish the same result: to get you to lower the standard which the other person does not like in order to avoid accountability. Unfortunately, too many of us fall for it. As a result, too many relationships or organizations are overthrown.

However, if you can name the game, you don't have to play it. I will often have to identify the games people are trying to play with me. But, if I can name the game that person is playing, it is amazing how quickly that game disappears.

ASSUMING YOUR BEST VERBAL JEET STANCE

Just like with any martial arts style, whenever you find yourself in a situation where you might need to defend yourself, you need to assume your best fighting stance. The same is true whenever you find yourself in a highly emotional conflict situation—you need your best Verbal Jeet stance.

My wife once told me that she can always tell when I am going to use Verbal Jeet with somebody. "You always do the same thing. You sit back, fold your arms, and then cock your head to the side."

"You mean like this?" I asked her. I sat back on my shoulders, slouched a bit, folded my arms, smiled a little, raised my eyebrows, and cocked my head to the right.

"Yeah, that's it," she told me.

I have done this so many times that I don't even think about it anymore. By now, it is pure habit. My wife's comment made me think about why I assumed this pose in preparation of conflict. I remember that when I first thought of the Verbal Jeet System, I knew that I had to make myself as comfortable as possible to keep my heart rate down. I needed to stay relaxed so my heart rate did not go above 145 beats per minute. If a human's heart rate tops 145 beats per minute, game over. We have a fight-or-flight response and our blood is rerouted out of our frontal lobes and into our arms, legs, and lungs. That reaction is always going to be bad for me. But if I can remain calm, I will be able to remain in control of my emotional system and let my logical brain take charge.

That is the essence of emotional intelligence: *Retaining control of your brain.*

I soon discovered that I could control myself much better when I sit in my specific Verbal Jeet stance, and then just chill.

Assuming my Verbal Jeet stance also helps to put the other person at ease. If I remain calm and relaxed then that other person will most likely stay more relaxed and their heart rate will also remain under 145 beats per minute. This tends to keep a lot of the tension out of the room.

You want to send positive nonverbals because all human beings have "mirror neurons" in their brains, which means the other person will most likely naturally mirror what you are doing.[93] If you look aggressive and lean in towards them, they tend to do the same thing to you. If you stay relaxed, they tend to do the same thing. This is also why if you yawn in a meeting, others will soon follow. I suggest you use these mirror neurons to your advantage and keep the atmosphere as calm and relaxed as possible.

Everyone needs to think about how they should position themselves in highly emotional conflicts to remain as calm and in control as possible. Then, everyone needs to practice using their Verbal Jeet move again and again. Eventually, you will do it automatically.

That will become your standard Verbal Jeet stance.

VERBAL JEET COACHING PROCESS

Whenever you find yourself in a high stakes conflict, this is the process you want to follow:

Problem Recognition Stage

The goal in the Problem Recognition Stage is to get the person to recognize that there is a problem to solve as soon as possible. You cannot solve anything unless all of the parties see that there is indeed a problem. The sooner you can get everyone to recognize that there is a real problem, the sooner you can get to the Problem-Solving Stage and you can work on solving the problem together.

1. Empathic listening

If the person doesn't know why they are there to meet with you or why you have come to see them, tell them. Then ask for their perspective, get into your best Verbal Jeet stance, and shut up! Listen carefully, because you are going to have to parrot all of what they say back to the other person's satisfaction.

Ways to initiate a conflict discussion include:

- "I wanted to touch base with you because I get the feeling that you are really upset with me and I am not sure why. If something is wrong, I want to fix it so we are good. Why don't you tell me what is going on?"
- "Your manager asked me to come see you because I understand there is a problem with this project. I want to hear your perspective because I want to see what we can do to fix this."
- "I understand you posted something on Facebook about how much you hate people of different religions. I looked at the post and wanted to hear from you why you did that."
- "I understand you have been saying that the company doesn't care about you anymore and we want you gone. Let's work this out. What's going on?"
- "I understand you told your manager that he was too stupid for his job. Well, I will tell you. That is going to be a problem. Why don't you tell me what you were thinking?"

I then assume my standard Verbal Jeet stance. I want to be able to breathe deeply and remain in control. I will often take notes, but I will also make eye contact and encourage the other person to talk at the same time. Just because I am taking some notes does not mean I can ignore the other person. I need to really focus my attention and be respectful … which is EPR. I am talking to a human right now, the most fickle, most emotional, most dangerous animal on the planet. A human can turn on you in a 17,000th of a second. Never forget that.

Making nonthreatening eye contact is important and respectful. I am showing that person I am focused solely on them. I will also nod my head and give the other person several "Rewards" as they talk. I want the other person to relax and tell me their story. I will typically say things like:

- "Okay."
- "Sure, I can see that."
- "I understand."
- "I see where you are coming from."

If you don't at least try to address and resolve the conflict, I have found that passive-aggressive people are going to stab you in the back regardless. It is in your best interest to address the problem and force the other side's hand to resolve it and hopefully improve your relationship. Otherwise, the situation you failed to address will only get worse.

2. Parrot it all back

Once the other person has told me their side, I will say something like: "Okay. Now, let me make sure I've got this. You're saying that…" If the person agrees that I understand, we move on to the "Rewards." However, if I misstate something and they correct me, we start over. We do not move on in the conversation until the other person agrees that I truly do understand their side.

3. "Reward"

If this person explains their side and I change my mind, the other person will be happy. People are not going to get upset when you agree with them. They get upset when we disagree with them. Of course, if that person has not changed my mind and I still disagree with them, I need to give that other person a reward. Again, giving someone a reward does not mean that you agree with that person's opinion or point of view. Giving someone a "Reward" means you are validating that person's point of view. You are acknowledging that you understand why they said what they said, why they did what they did, and why they feel the way they do. However, it certainly does not mean that you are agreeing with the other person, only that you understand their position.

I would then say something like: "I understand what you are telling me and why you feel that way, but you cannot make those types of comments to others." Unfortunately, this is where people often play games with us. We spend the first five or six years of our lives learning how to play these games, and then the next 70 to 80 years trying to perfect them.

Just remember: if you can name the game, you don't have to play it.

4. **If it appears as if the other person is at fault, then make sure the person is held accountable**

    a. Make sure the person understands that the problem exists.

The person may agree that the standard is not being met, but insists it is not their fault. If the person does not take accountability, then depending on the situation, there are some keys to use to address their defenses.

> **Key:** What if everybody did this?

If the person does not think what they are doing is a big deal, ask them:

- "What if everybody was five minutes late?"
- "What if everybody left five minutes early?"
- "What if everybody missed these types of mistakes?"

It is hard to ask for special treatment when you take a personal issue and expand it to be a universal issue. I have found this key to be very useful at the right times whenever someone is breaking the rules but does not want to comply. If the person is a Retreater, then ask the person:

> **Key:** "Do you think saying these things behind their back is going to solve anything … other than make you look bad?""

Again, Retreaters do what they do because they think they are being "nice." They want people to like them. So, whenever I coach a Retreater, it is important to remind the person that when others find out that they are not being honest, they will be seen as "untrustworthy." They will be disliked. This tends to help them see what they are really doing.

Also, I always ask them if they think talking behind someone's back is really going to solve anything? You cannot resolve an issue if you don't address it.

Next, if the person did something offensive, but does not think what they did was a big deal, just ask them:

Key: "What would the 'reasonable person' think if this was on the front page of *USA Today*?"

(This is actually the test for determining "What is Offensive" and "Hypersensitivity" from the United States Supreme Court's decision, *Harris v. Forklift Systems*, 510 U.S. 17 (1993). So, you have been living under this standard for a few decades now … whether you knew it or not.)

For instance, I have had to ask such questions as:

- "What if the naked selfie you took was on the front page of *USA Today*? What would most people think?"
- "What if a picture of you mooning your co-worker was on the front page of *USA Today*? How would people react?"
- "What if a video of you cursing was on the front page of *USA Today's* website? What would most people say about you?"

This tends to bring a bit of reality back into the picture.

So, whenever I run into someone who just did something really stupid, I ask that person: "What would a reasonable person think if this was on the front page of *USA Today*?" They usually smile and see the light.

Next, whenever I have to coach someone who is bullying a co-worker or a supervisor who is bullying an employee, I will ask them,

Key: "Would you treat a customer like that?" or "Would you treat the CEO like that?"

If the person bullied someone or acted like an Attacker towards a coworker, ask them if they would treat a customer like that. *Remember:* customer service is nothing more than employee relations turned outward. Employee relations is nothing more than customer service turned inward. The exact same Verbal Jeet Skills we use to resolve conflict with employees are the exact same skills we use to resolve conflicts with customers. It is amazing to me how often organizations think it's okay to let employees and managers be rude and dismissive to each other, but then demand these same employees give superior customer service to the clientele. It is hypocritical. The bottom line is: you treat your employees like customers and vice versa.

b. Inform the person that this is their problem to solve, not yours.

You cannot solve other people's problems for them. That is their job and their problem to solve. When we have these discussions with employees, it is their job to meet the standard that you set. Your job is to help them meet your standard. If they are at fault, it is their problem to solve, not yours. The other person must take accountability in order to achieve the desired result. Your job might be to help that person, but you cannot make anyone improve. They must do it. Of course, if you have some fault here, you need to take accountability as well and improve. Too often, we work harder to solve the problem than they do. That simply cannot and will not work.

Remind the other person of the standard that is expected of them as compared to what they are currently doing. Explain the detrimental effect this problem may have, or has had, on the person, the department, and the company. If the person can see where they were wrong, you can move out of the Problem Recognition Stage and on to the Problem Resolution Stage. This is where you can partner up with the other person and work on the problem together.

Of course, if the person does not take any accountability for what they are doing wrong, you cannot move on to the Problem Resolution Stage. No one will fix a problem when they don't see a problem to solve.

Problem-Solving Stage

Once the other person recognizes that there is a problem to solve, you can move to the Problem-Solving Stage. This is where everyone can work on solving the problem together.

Of course, sometimes, you never get this far. The other person may refuse to recognize that a problem exists, or sometimes the person refuses to take responsibility. That most likely signals the end of the relationship.

Again, you are not God. You cannot make anyone do anything.

Magic Bullet: "How can I help you?"

5.   The key to problem solving lies in helping that other person improve.

I stole the phrase, "How can I help you" from the Americans With Disabilities Act. Whenever you run into a person with a disability, it really doesn't matter what condition the person has contracted. ALL that matters is what do you need to do to help this person. That is it.

So, whenever you encounter an ADA issue with someone, you sit down with that person and ask: "How can I help you?"

This is exactly the same question you ask in coaching. It works just as well in a non-ADA situation because it shows a concern to help the other person with a problem. Actually, if you are ever coaching someone and you don't know what to say, just ask: "How can I help you?" or "What can I do to help you?"

It is a *magic bullet.*
Never hesitate to use your magic bullet!

6.   Discuss possible solutions to the problem. Adopt the most viable ones as goals.
     Partner up and devise a plan to alleviate the problem and meet these goals.

You cannot make anyone do anything. This is not your job—it is the other person's. Your job is to help this person reach their goals. *Remember:* if you say you are going to do something, you must do it. If the other person says they are going to do something, hold them accountable.

7.   Agree on the right course of action and the appropriate follow-up measures to be taken.

Get the other person to agree to take accountability for this action plan. This is not your plan. It is the other person's plan to execute.

8.   Monitor progress in some manner and follow up with the other person.

9.   Recognize and/or reward achievement (positive feedback). Revisit the issue if improvement is not seen.

In order to make the Verbal Jeet Coaching Process a little easier to visualize, I have abbreviated it all into the single-page handout, found at the end of this chapter. I suggest you keep this page handy and refer to it often just to keep it all fresh in your minds.

FRANK AND RITA

I once represented an organization where, toward the beginning of summer one year, an organizational lunch was held in their cafeteria. The employees were all talking about their vacation plans for the summer. One group of women were sitting together talking about taking a trip together. They discussed maybe going to a beach, which is a common vacation getaway. However, one man, Frank, thought this discussion was also a good time to make fun of the weight of some of the women in the room. (Oh, yeah. That will win you lots of friends.)

Frank made comments like: "What are you going to call this trip? The great whaling expedition?" and "Boy, it is really going to be hard to tell the difference between some of the women out there and beached whales."

As Frank continued to speak, the women in the room grew more and more angry. You could see it as their bodies shifted in their seats. Their shoulders stiffened and their eyes began to pierce through Frank.

Clearly, he was not paying any attention to the dozens of nonverbal cues in the room. He was mind blind. Eventually, one woman, Rita, got up from her chair, got herself a cup of hot coffee, calmly walked over to Frank, and poured it on his head.

Most of the women in the room applauded. It was at this point that I got a call from my client. I scheduled appointments to see both Frank and Rita. When I first met Frank, he was really angry. Rita had scalded his head and shoulders with piping hot coffee. He couldn't wait to tell me his story. This is where I used my Verbal Jeet Coaching Process.

FRANK

Verbal Jeet Coaching Process
Problem Recognition Stage
The goal in the Problem Recognition Stage is to get the person to recognize that there is a problem to solve as soon as possible. You cannot solve anything

unless all of the parties see that there is indeed a problem. The sooner you can get everyone to recognize that there is a real problem, the sooner you can get to the Problem-Solving Stage and you can work on solving the problem together.

1. Empathic listening

I started my conversation with Frank by saying, "Frank I wanted to talk to you about what happened with Rita. The company does not want to fire you, but they did ask me to come in to try and help "you." This is a version of the magic bullet: "What can I do to help you?" The people I coach always start out thinking that I am brought in to get them. I have to gain their trust, which means they know it is safe to talk to me and that I mean them no harm.

I then explained, "Your manager told me his side, but I wanted to hear it from you and get your perspective. Why don't you tell me what happened?"

I then got into my standard Verbal Jeet stance. Again, I like to sit back on my shoulders, slouch a bit, fold my arms, smile, raise my eyebrows in a cooperative fashion, cock my head to the right, and listen. I want to slow the pace of the session down and create as much of a relaxed environment as possible.

Frank started off talking very fast, which is always bad for a coaching session.

So, I stopped him and said, "It's okay. Just take a deep breath, slow down, relax, and tell me what happened. There is no reason to be nervous. Just talk to me. I need you to slow down so I can follow you. I just want to hear your side. It's all good."

Of course, when I told him all this, I slowed my speech way down. I continued to slouch on my shoulders. I looked as chilled as I could.

Frank took a deep breath, paused for a minute, got a drink of water, and said. "Okay." He continued at a much slower pace, "You see, these women always get together in their little group and talk about everyone else. They have their own little opinions about everyone. It is so irritating how they think they are better than everyone else."

While Frank was talking, I continued to nod my head in encouragement and gave him some encouragers ("Rewards"). I wanted him to relax and tell me his story. I would say things like:

- "Okay."
- "Sure, I can see that."
- "I understand."
- "I see where you are coming from."

Frank then said these women were all talking about going to the beach, and it struck him as being really funny. "They all picture themselves as being so 'high and mighty,'" he told me. He then pictured all these women out on the beach with their sun tan lotion and big straw hats. He thought that was just hilarious.

2. *Parrot it all back*

I then told Frank, "Okay. Now, let me make sure I've got this. You're saying that these women have their own little group and they all sit together at lunch. They don't let anyone else join them. They often talk about everyone else at the office and think they are better than everyone else. And that really ticks you off. Is that right?"

"Well, yeah. They just all think they are something special," Frank replied.

"Okay. So, when they started talking about going to Hilton Head together, you pictured them in their bathing suits and thought that looked funny. Right?" I asked.

Frank then started laughing and said, "Well, yeah! Have you seen them? Why would they all go to a beach somewhere?"

3. *"Reward"*

Because Frank acknowledged that I did understand his side, and because he did not change my mind about what he said, I told Frank,

"Okay. I understand what you are telling me and why you feel that way, but you cannot make those types of comments to other people. It is very offensive."

Frank instantly said, "So, that gives Rita the right to pour hot coffee on me?"

"No, not at all," I told Frank.

Frank was playing a little bit of the Diversion game here, which meant he was telling me to "look over there" and blame Rita. I told him that what Rita did was wrong and that I was going to talk to her next, but that we are not talking about Rita right now—we are talking about his comments.

Frank then started playing the Victim game. "So, I make a few comments and now I'm in trouble?"

"Well," I asked Frank. "What do you think most people would think if your comments were on the front page of *USA Today*?"

"I don't know. I don't think it is that big of a deal," Frank told me.

"Really? Why don't you read these statements out loud to me?" I asked him. I handed Frank my notes that had his statements written down. Frank looked at the list and read silently for a minute.

"Go ahead. Read them out loud," I said.

Frank then started to read his statements out loud.

"What are you going to call this trip? The great whaling expedition?" he read, smiling.

"Go ahead," I said mockingly. " Why don't you read the one about why whales really beach themselves?"

"No, I get it. These are probably offensive. But these were just a few isolated jokes," Frank said.

"Would you make those same jokes to your boss? Or to a customer?" I asked.

"No, of course not," he replied.

"Then what makes you think that it's okay to say these things to an employee—the biggest part of your budget and the people who execute your strategic plans?" I asked. "See, Frank," I told him. "You are just playing games with me. We're not going to do that here. Deep down, you know the truth. We're going to solve the problem and get you back on the right track. You can't solve any problem if you cannot see where things went wrong."

When I met him, Frank was paying a very heavy price for his behavior at work and in his personal life. He could not really sustain long-term relationships with anyone. This is a typical scenario. Everywhere Frank went, he took himself with him.

4. *If it appears as if the other person is at fault, then make sure the person is held accountable.*

Clearly, Frank saw this was a problem, but he was still trying to downplay these "few isolated jokes," as he described them.

I reminded Frank of the organization's standard. "Our standard here is that you don't engage in behavior that would likely offend a reasonable person in the community. That is also the legal standard we are forced to follow, whether we like it or not. In other words, if this was on the front page of *USA Today*, what would most people think? This is an important standard because we all have to work with each other. In other words, you don't do or say anything you wouldn't be proud to have on the front page of a newspaper."

"But they were only a few jokes. Come on," Frank told me.

"Okay. What if everybody made just a few comments like that? What if everyone did that to each other just once a year?" I asked him. With that, Frank was cornered. Even though Rita overreacted to his comments, he was way out of line in what he said, and he knew it.

Because Frank could now see where he was wrong, we could move out of the Problem Recognition Stage and on to the Problem Resolution Stage. This is where we can partner up and work on the problem together. Of course, if Frank had not taken any accountability for what he had done, there is no reason to move on to the Problem-Solving Stage. No one will fix a problem when they don't see any problem to solve.

Problem-Solving Stage
5. *Discuss possible solutions to the problem. Adopt the most viable ones as goals. Partner up and devise a plan to alleviate the problem and meet these goals.*

Frank and I then looked at his EQ scores, because I obviously had him take an EQ Assessment. Frank scored very low in the areas of "Emotional Awareness," "Self-Regard" and "Interpersonal Relationships." Clearly,

Frank did not feel good about himself, so he was primed to see others as looking down on him and excluding him, which might not be the case at all. Further, Frank had trouble getting along with others and building relationships.

I used my magic bullet phrase as soon as we got to the Problem-Solving Stage. As we looked over his scores, I said to him: "What can I do to help *you?*"

I told him "I am not here to hurt you. I was brought in to help you. Let's put together a plan that will help you improve these scores and get you back on the right track."

Together, we developed the following strategies for Frank to adopt over the next few weeks:

- Realize your strengths and be aware of weaknesses, but do not obsess over them. Write them down. Take your time. Set plans and goals for improving weaknesses. Take charge.
- Articulate what bothers you by actually saying it out loud to yourself. Consciously ask yourself, "Why did I react or feel that way?" after an intense interaction. Maybe you should record yourself and listen to the playback later.
- Keep a diary or journal and write down these emotions and feelings.
- Identify your "hot spots" and why they are there.
- Get a sounding board. Ask what impact your actions are having on others.
- Take part in more group activities, either at work or in your private life.

I also referred Frank to the company's Employee Assistance Program (EAP) to be assessed. EAPs can be very useful as professional sounding boards and for identifying any deeper issues.

I finally recommended that he get a physical and a full fasting blood work test. This is just a good idea to make sure his body is functioning properly. There have been many times where behavior issues were caused by some unknown physical problems, such as diabetes, high blood pressure, or thyroid issues. Considering Frank's off-the-wall comments, I thought there might be something else going on that would make him act in such an inappropriate manner.

Remember: Your brain controls everything you do. So, if you have uncontrolled diabetes, or a thyroid problem, your behavior could very easily turn bizarre. It is important to remember that there is no difference between brain health and your behavior, so whenever I coach someone like Frank, they need to get some blood work done first and foremost.

6. Agree on the right course of action and the appropriate follow-up measures to be taken.

Frank liked the plan and the strategies we set out, largely because it was his plan. We worked on it together. I gave him suggestions and he decided if it was something that he could do or not.

Always remember: "The process is more important than the product."

This means that you never just impose an improvement plan on anyone. You work on it together. The other person has to have input or it never really becomes their plan. When people work on something and help to build it, they tend to take more responsibility for it.

This plan also gave Frank some specific actions to focus on, rather than just hitting him in the head and saying, "Do better," which never works.

7. Monitor progress in some manner and follow up with the employee.

I told Frank to call me in four weeks. We could discuss how things were going. What worked and what did not. I told Frank that I would be following up with his human resource director and manager to see how it was all going. Everyone was on the same team. His development is a group effort.

Remember: if you say you are going to do something, you must do it.

8. Recognize and/or reward achievement (Positive Feedback).

If Frank ended up doing well, I would complement him and maybe give him some additional strategies. Progress is what we are looking for here. If he can take the pain of admitting he has an issue, he will most likely improve.

In the end, Frank did very well. He became much more self-aware and his social skills improved remarkably—even with the organization's clients.

Remember: the exact same skills we all use to interact with our employees are the exact same skills we use to interact with our families and our clients.

These are not just "work skills." Verbal Jeet is a life skill.

RITA

It was then time to meet with Rita. When I first met with her, I could see that she was very nervous. So, I had to put her at ease. I started my meeting by introducing myself and telling her, "I have been speaking with Tom, your HR director. But I wanted to hear everything from you."

I then used a version of my magic bullet: "I am here to help you. Does that make sense?"

A sense of relief shone through Rita's face as she quietly agreed, smiled a little bit, and said she understood. Clearly, she did not entirely believe me. She was still very cautious, but that is okay. I would just have to prove it to her in this meeting.

Again, as always, I used my typical Verbal Jeet move and said, "Okay, then why don't you just relax and tell me what happened." Rita then went through her side of everything that happened in the lunchroom that day. As I sat and listened, I encouraged her to continue talking by nodding and giving her a few "Rewards" by saying things like "Uh-huh," "I understand," "I see," and so on.

When she finished telling me her story, I leaned forward and said, "Okay, now let me make sure I got all of this straight…" and went through her side. I parroted back to her everything that she told me from her perspective until she agreed that I understood. I also parroted back to Rita how these comments made her feel and what she was thinking as Frank insulted her and her friends. It was clear this was a highly emotional issue for her. It was important that I understand and acknowledge her feelings. She agreed that I understood how those comments made her feel.

Actually, when I acknowledged her feelings, her eyes brightened and she leaned into me and said, "Yeah, that's right. It really bothered me." Of course, only after Rita agreed that I understood the facts as she saw them and how she felt about what had happened did we move on. Once we had this agreement, I was done with parroting.

It was then time to reward her point of view because she had not changed my mind that she was unjustified in pouring coffee on Frank. Assault is never the right decision to make when trying to resolve a conflict. I told Rita, "I understand why you did what you did. In fact, I would bet that most of the women in the room, would have wanted to do the same thing to Frank—but you can't do things like that. Yes, you had every right to be offended. In fact, if what Frank did was on the front page of *USA Today*, I think most people would be shocked. However, there is no such thing as 'justifiable assault.' You can't dump hot coffee on someone because you're ticked off at him. Now you have lowered yourself to his level. Had you not done that to Frank, he would have been the only one I would be talking to today. Now you get to meet with me, too. Do you understand what I mean by all this?"

"Yes, I do," Rita said. "I know it was a stupid thing to do, but I was just so upset over all of it."

"I understand," I told her. "That's your emotional system hijacking your brain. Your logic went out the window and your emotions took over. It happens to all of us, but we all have to get better at controlling it. We've all punched walls and kicked our cars. Those are dumb things to do. That is why we need to work together. We need to figure out what you need to do when you feel this way so it doesn't happen again. You need to stop and think to yourself, 'How much do I want to contribute to my own misery?'"

She smiled a bit. She knew what she did was wrong. It was an emotional outburst and one that cannot happen again. She got it. Because she accepted her role in this, we could start problem-solving together.

I told her that rather than pouring hot coffee on Frank, she could have told Frank that she was really offended by his comments and he needed to stop. If she felt she did not have enough control over herself to do that, then she could have left the room and reported him. She could have gone to management. We examined other methods of dealing with her anger, rather than with hot coffee.

I had Rita write down our brainstorming ideas. I wasn't going to write them down because it was not my plan. It was Rita's plan. She was the one who needed to improve.

Slowing down and thinking was the key. I drew her a quick picture of how the brain's emotional system works and why her frontal lobes basically shut down on her. I have found that understanding how our brain works, more specifically our emotional system and our logical system, helps people to not only visualize why they are reacting the way they are, but helps them to better control it.

I also referred her to a specialist through the company's EAP to use as a sounding board and to be assessed for possible underlying issues.

I did not think Rita's issues were as severe as Frank's. That is why I did not think it was necessary to have her get her blood work done. I did not test her EQ. However, she did snap, and even though one could easily see why she did that, that cannot ever happen again. I felt just talking to someone could help her get a better handle on why she assaulted Frank … and how she could avoid that in the future.

Note: You never want to send someone for "treatment." That violates the Americans With Disabilities Act because you are regarding them as being disabled. You send them to be "assessed" by a trained health care provider. If the health care provider recommends treatment, the employee can be required to follow the provider's recommendations. I might know "weird" when I see it, like with Frank, but I cannot diagnose other people. That is illegal. Health care providers do that.

I also gave Rita some basic EI strategies to follow, similar to the ones I gave Frank. Even though I did not give Rita an EQ Assessment, it was obvious she has certain triggers she needed to get under control.

By the time we were done, Rita understood my message and agreed with me.

This is how we deal with highly emotional situations. Such high stakes poker situations will make or break our most important relationships. Treating others with respect by starting with Empathic Listening, Parroting, and "Rewards" will do a great deal to create and preserve the trust in the relationship. This also allows trust to grow because the other person knows it is safe to speak up.

It is also vital that we reassure this person that we are there to help them. Because we are coaching them, we want them to improve. They have to understand that we are not there to hurt them, and that this is for their development. So, whenever you are not sure what to say, which will always happen in a coaching situation, just pull out your magic bullet and ask "How can I help you?" or "What can I do to help you?" or "I am here to help you."

When we were done, Rita knew I really was not there to do her any harm. I was there to try and help her make her life better. We have a very good relationship now. She trusts me.

THE DREADED GOSSIPERS

I am always flabbergasted when I hear someone say that you just can't do anything about gossipers. They talk about everyone and everything behind their backs, including the company, and spread their emotional venom and negativity everywhere. Management is usually very hesitant to say anything to gossipers because they heard about the gossip through the grapevine. First of all, the grapevine is accurate—some say about 80 percent accurate.[94] Not only is it very accurate, it is faster than any memo management will ever send out.

The grapevine is also made up of people. It is not some mystical information source where the walls whisper secrets to you. Your employees and the people you know make up the grapevine. We usually hear about gossip from a trusted source who heard the information first hand. Unfortunately, I will often hear from HR and management that they cannot rely on what they hear from other employees because it's "hearsay." I consider this mindset ridiculous, and unfortunately, I hear it all the time. What you hear from trusted sources is not hearsay. Hearsay only occurs in court, like if I were to testify to what someone saw, when that exact person was actually sitting in the room and able to act as a witness themselves.

Instead, when employees tell you "I saw that" or "I heard this" directly from the source, that is what we call "direct evidence." Management has every right to rely on direct evidence. You have to rely on the input of your trusted people. No one robs a store when a cop is sitting in the parking lot. Likewise, few people are going to bad mouth the company when management is standing right there. If you let gossipers continue bad-mouthing the company behind your back, you are actually giving them tacit approval to continue.

However, if you bring the person in to discuss the issue, you can try to resolve it. As a result, you will soon get the reputation that you are not going to let problems fester. Instead, you are going to bring the people in and try to address the issue.

This is the reputation you want:

> I will never attack you. I will also never talk about you behind your back. Instead, whenever I have a problem, I will come and see you and we will resolve it.

I deal with this issue all the time—and my Verbal Jeet Skills save me.

I once had a client where the backstabbing and vicious gossiping about the company was rampant. I asked the HR manager to give me some examples.

They told me about Phyllis. Phyllis was a long-time employee who talked about others behind their backs. She was a typical Retreater, like most of us. I was told that Phyllis had been complaining about the new work schedules. Apparently, the company had just picked up a new large customer who was in a later time zone. As a result, the company now had to cover longer customer service hours in order to service them.

I called in Phyllis to see me. The HR manager was sitting beside me when she came in because I wanted Phyllis to see that she could trust them, too. I also thought it was important for HR to see how Verbal Jeet Skills work in real life.

When Phyllis came into the room, I got out of my chair and shook her hand. She was familiar with me because I had already conducted some training at the company on conflict resolution.

"It's good to see you again," I said and then I assumed my best Verbal Jeet stance.

"I understand that the new schedule has a lot of people upset," I told her.

"Yes, I guess some people are upset," she said. She really wanted to get out of the room when I said this, but that was not going to happen.

"I also understand that you are not too happy about it, either," I told her.

"Who told you that?" she asked a bit angrily.

"That isn't important," I told her. "What I want to do is hear where you are coming from and see if we can help you." (Magic bullet time!)

She started to explain that the staff was not given much time to adjust to the new schedule and it was interfering with picking up and dropping off her kids at school.

"Yeah, I could see how that could cause some problems," I told her. (A reward.) "Let me get this straight. This new schedule was imposed on you in about a week and has caused a lot of trouble for you—one of which is working out the drop off and pick up schedule for your kids," I repeated to her.

"Well, yes, among other things," she told me.

"Then help me understand the scope of what is happening here. What other problems has this caused that we could maybe help you with?" I asked.

Then … the massive list started. This was going to take a while. Phyllis rattled off a host of problems that she and other staff members had encountered. I repeated them all back to her to make sure I understood. She said that I did.

I started going through her list one at a time with the HR manager. I told her I understood where she was coming from, and I did. It doesn't seem like that it was that long ago when my kids were in school and my wife and I had to juggle pick-ups and drops-offs.

Some of the things she mentioned the company could not do anything about. However, we still discussed and reasoned through them with her so she understood the pressures being put on the company. I asked her what she would suggest the company do to help with these problems. She didn't have any suggestions. She was just upset with the situation, which is common. However, asking someone "How can we help you?" not only shows concern, but puts the responsibility of coming up with solutions on the employee. Again, the process is more important than the product. In other words, the final decision is not as important as letting the people most affected by it help find solutions.

However, some of the issues she brought up could be addressed. The HR manager was very helpful in suggesting some alternatives where the company could work around certain pick-up and drop off times, as well as some suggestions about how the company could address some of the other issues Phyllis was raising.

By the end of the meeting, Phyllis was all smiles. She was included in the process. Some things were better, but most remained the same. Still, she had her say, we listened to her, and she understood why the company had certain policies in place.

I told Phyllis, "You know, if you have any issues in the future, you need to come see us. We can't fix what we don't know about. We have to start talking to each other around here."

Phyllis nodded.

"And if you hear someone else who is having problems, encourage them to come to HR so we can address what is happening," I said.

Hopefully, in the future, she will come and see HR before joining in on the gossiping. However, doing this one time with one gossiper will not completely solve the issue. To get people to come to you, you have to go through this process several times. You need to use your Verbal Jeet Skills and show everyone that it is safe to discuss difficult topics with you. You can use conflicts to show other people that you do not mean them any harm, and that builds trust and relationships.

You can prove to them that it is "safe" to talk to you. *That* is trust. However, it takes a long time to build trust … and only seconds to destroy it.

In most disagreements, both sides usually share many common beliefs and opinions. However, when our emotions take over, we cannot see where we agree with one another. All we can see is our anger and where we disagree. So, our emotions overtake our logic and make decisions for us in 17,000ths of a second.

That is usually not good.

Solutions stem from our mutual interests and goals. That is where we find our common ground—and when we can see where the true common ground lies, solutions emerge.

That is the reason we all need to work harder at becoming emotionally intelligent and using our Verbal Jeet Skills.

VERBAL JEET COACHING PROCESS

Problem Recognition Stage

1. Empathic Listening

   If the person doesn't know why they are there, tell them. Then ask them their side, assume your best Verbal Jeet stance, and shut up!

2. Parrot it all back

   "Okay. Now, let me make sure I've got this. You're saying that…"

3. "Reward"

   "I understand what you are saying and why you feel that way, but you cannot make those types of comments to others. It is very offensive."

4. If it appears that the other person is at fault, make sure they are held accountable.

   a. Make sure the person understands that the problem exists.

      Key: What if everybody did this?

      Key: "What would a reasonable person think if this was on the front page of *USA Today*?

      Key: "Would you treat a customer or the CEO like that?" (If the person was being an Attacker)

      Key: "Do you think saying these things behind their back is going to solve anything other than make you look bad?" (If the person was being a Retreater)

   b. Now inform the person that this is their problem to solve, not yours.

      If the person can see where he was wrong, you can move out of the Problem Recognition Stage and move on to the Problem Resolution Stage.

Problem Resolution Stage

Magic Bullet: "How can I help you?"

5. Discuss possible solutions to the problem. Adopt the most viable ones as goals. Partner up and devise a plan to alleviate the problem and meet these goals.

6. Agree on the right course of action and the appropriate follow-up measures to be taken.

7. Monitor progress in some manner and follow up with the other person.

8. Recognize and/or reward achievement (positive feedback). Revisit the issue if improvement is not seen.

Endnotes

INTRODUCTION

1. "The EEOC's Fiscal Year 2018 Highlights," U. S. Equal Employment Opportunity Commission, accessed April 25, 2019, https://www.eeoc.gov/eeoc/newsroom/wysk/2018_highlights.cfm.

CHAPTER 1. WHY EMOTIONAL INTELLIGENCE?

2. "Meeting Tibetans in Minneapolis and Travelling on to Boston," The Office of His Holiness the Dalai Lama, June 24, 2017, https://www.dalailama.com/news/2017/meeting-tibetans-in-minneapolis-and-travelling-on-to-boston.

3. Tom Peters, *Tom Peters: The Power of Excellence, The Forgotten Customer*, aired March 17, 1987, on PBS.

4. "Pete Rose Stats," Baseball-Reference.com, accessed April 25, 2019, https://www.baseball-reference.com/players/r/rosepe01.shtml. See also Wikipedia, s.v. "Pete Rose," last modified April 25, 2019, 04:00 (UTC), https://en.wikipedia.org/wiki/Pete_Rose.

5. Daniel Goleman, *Emotional Intelligence* (New York: Bantam, 1995), 34. See also Daniel Goleman, *Working With Emotional Intelligence* (New York: Bantam, 1998), 19.

6. Travis Bradberry and Jean Greaves, The Emotional Intelligence Quick Book (New York: Fireside, 2005), 39, 53.

7. Goleman, *Working With Emotional Intelligence*, 31.

8. Goleman, 31.

9. Goleman, 34, 42–43, 187.

10. Bradberry and Greaves, *The Emotional Intelligence Quick Book*, 43.

11. Goleman, *Working With Emotional Intelligence*, 5.

12. Bradberry and Greaves, *Emotional Intelligence Quick Book*, 25.

CHAPTER 2. NEUROLOGY OF EMOTIONAL INTELLIGENCE

13. Daniel Goleman, *Emotional Intelligence: Why It Can Matter More Than IQ* (New York: Bantam, 1995), 7.

14. Goleman, 7.

15. Goleman, 15, 18–20.

16. Daniel Goleman, *Social Intelligence: The New Science of Human Relationships* (New York: Bantam, 2006), 40.

17. Goleman, *Emotional Intelligence*, 14–18.

18. Goleman, 14-18.

19. Joseph LeDoux, *Synaptic Self: How Our Brains Become Who We Are* (New York: Penguin Books, 2003), 15-20. See also Goleman, *Social Intelligence*, 16, 40, 268.

20. Goleman, *Social Intelligence*, 16, 40.
21. Goleman, 22–24, 91, 98.
22. Goleman, 16, 40.
23. Ralph Adolphs, "What Does the Amygdala Contribute to Social Cognition?," *Annals of the New York Academy of Sciences* 1191, no. 1: 42–61, accessed May 15, 2010, https://www.ncbi.nlm.nih.gov/pmc/articles/PMC2871162/.
24. Goleman, *Emotional Intelligence*, 15.
25. Ryan Hamilton, *How You Decide: The Science of Human Decision Making* (Chantilly: The Teaching Company, 2016), 33.
26. Daniel Amen, *Healing the Hardware of the Soul: How Making the Brain-Soul Connection Can Optimize Your Life, Love, and Spiritual Growth* (New York: The Free Press, 2002), 31. See also Hamilton, *How You Decide*, 33.
27. Amen, 19. See also Daniel Amen, *Magnificent Mind at Any Age: Natural Ways to Unleash Your Brain's Maximum Potential* (Easton: Harmony Press, 2008), 13.
28. Amen, *Magnificent Mind at Any Age*, 31–32.
29. Amen, 31–32.
30. Amen, 31–32.
31. Amen, 31–32.
32. Travis Bradberry and Jean Greaves, *The Emotional Intelligence Quick Book* (New York: Fireside, 2005), 120–21. See also Goleman, *Emotional Intelligence*, 26.
33. Bradberry and Greaves, 120–21.
34. Hamilton, *How You Decide,* 34–37.
35. Hamilton, 34–37.
36. Hamilton, 34–37.
37. United States Department of Labor, Occupational Safety and Health Administration, "Workplace Violence," accessed January 28, 2017.
38. Goleman, *Social Intelligence*, 40.
39. Malcolm Gladwell, *Blink: The Power of Thinking Without Thinking* (New York: Little, Brown and Company, 2005), 224–28.
40. Gladwell, 224–28. Dr. Keith Payne, Assistant Professor of Psychology at the University of North Carolina, claims we become "temporarily autistic" in such situations. "In short, we simply shut down and focus only on the immediate task at hand … blocking out all other external stimuli. Perspective abandons us, which can create a very dangerous situation."
41. Goleman, *Emotional Intelligence*, 139.
42. Daniel Goleman, *Working with Emotional Intelligence* (New York: Bantam, 1998), 60.
43. Goleman, *Social Intelligence*, 22–23, 40.
44. Goleman, 22–23, 40.
45. Goleman, 9, 66–67, 158.
46. Goleman, 66–67, 158.
47. Goleman, 66–67, 158.
48. Goleman, 66–67, 158.
49. Goleman, 66–67, 158. "While most all the hundreds of types on neurons in the human brain are found in other mammals, spindle cells are a rare exception. We share them only with our closest cousins, the apes. Orangutans, a distant relative, have a few hundred; our

closer genetic relatives the gorillas, chimps, and bonobos have far more. And we humans have the most, close to a hundred thousand of them."

50. Goleman, 66–67, 158.

51. Goleman, 16, 22–23, 40, 268.

52. Goleman, 16, 22–23, 40, 268.

53. Joseph LeDoux, *Synaptic Self: How Our Brains Become Who We Are* (New York: Penguin Books, 2003), 20. See also Goleman, *Social Intelligence*, 16, 22–23, 40, 268.

54. Goleman, *Emotional Intelligence*, 20.

55. Daniel Amen, *Change Your Brain, Change Your Body: Use Your Brain to Get and Keep the Body You Have Always Wanted* (Easton: Harmony Press, 2010), 18.

56. Delmar Hatesohl and Dick Lee, "Listening: Our Most Used Communications Skill," University of Missouri Extension, last reviewed October 1993, https://extension2.missouri.edu/cm150.

57. Hatesohl and Lee.

58. Goleman, *Emotional Intelligence*, 52–53.

59. Goleman, 52–53.

60. Goleman, 52–53.

61. Goleman, 52–53.

62. Goleman, 52–53.

63. Goleman, 52–53.

64. Goleman, 52–53.

65. Goleman, 52–53.

66. Goleman, 52–53.

67. Goleman, 52–53.

CHAPTER 3. THE GODFATHER EFFECT

68. Robert J. Sternberg, "Human Intelligence," in *Encyclopedia Britannica Online*, accessed May 13, 2019, https://www.britannica.com/science/human-intelligence-psychology.

69. Gladwell, *Blink*, 24.

70. Wikipedia, s.v. "Edward Thorndike," last modified February 20, 2019, https://en.wikipedia.org/wiki/Edward_Thorndike#cite_note-14.

71. "Edward Thorndike"

72. "Edward Thorndike"

73. "Edward Thorndike"

74. "Edward Thorndike"

75. "Edward Thorndike"

76. Goleman, *Working with Emotional Intelligence*, 34. See also Bradberry and Greaves, *The Emotional Intelligence Quick Book*, 53.

77. Eddie Erlandson and Kate Ludeman, "Coaching the Alpha Male," *Harvard Business Review,* May 2004.

78. Bradberry and Greaves, *The Emotional Intelligence Quick Book*, 36.

79. Bradberry and Greaves, 40.

80. Bradberry and Greaves, 40.

81. Bradberry and Greaves, 42–43.

82. Goleman, *Working with Emotional Intelligence*, 34. See also Bradberry and Greaves, *Emotional Intelligence Quick Book*, 53.

83. Goleman, 19, 320–21.

84. Goleman, 38.

85. Goleman, 38.

86. Goleman, 39.

87. Goleman, 219.

CHAPTER 5. THE THREE STYLES OF COMMUNICATION: RETREATERS, ATTACKERS, AND HONEST COMMUNICATORS

88. "32 Shocking Divorce Statistics," *McKinley Irvin* (blog), updated 2018, https://www.mckinleyirvin.com/family-law-blog/2012/october/32-shocking-divorce-statistics/.

89. Goleman, *Social Intelligence*, 218.

90. Bradberry and Greaves, *Emotional Intelligence Quick Book*, 143.

91. Sara Ganim, "Exclusive: Jerry Sandusky Interview Prompts Long-Ago Victims to Contact Lawyer," *The Patriot News,* November 17, 2011, http://www.pennlive.com/midstate/index.ssf/2011/11/exclusive_jerry_sandusky_inter.htm. See also The Associated Press, "Penn State Settlements Covered 1971 Sandusky Abuse Claim," *USA Today*, May 9, 2016, http://www.usatoday.com/story/sports/ncaaf/2016/05/08/penn-state-settlements-jerry-sandusky-joe-paterno/84125254/.

92. Ganim, "Exclusive: Jerry Sandusky Interview." See also The Associated Press, "Penn State Settlements."

CHAPTER 9. THE VERBAL JEET COACHING PROCESS

93. Goleman, *Social Intelligence*, 91.

94. Jitendra Mishra, "Excerpts from … Managing the Grapevine," Analytic Technologies, http://www.analytictech.com/mb119/grapevine-article.htm. Article originally published in Public Personnel Management 19, no. 2 (June 1, 1990).

Bibliography

Aristotle. *Nicomachean Ethics.* Translated by Harris Rackham. Loeb Classical Library 73. Cambridge: Harvard University Press, 1999.

Adolphs, Ralph. "What Does the Amygdala Contribute to Social Cognition?" *Annals of the New York Academy of Sciences* 1191, no. 1 (2010): 42-61. doi:10.1111/j.1749-6632.2010.05445.x.

Amen, Daniel G. *Change Your Brain, Change Your Body: Use Your Brain to Get and Keep the Body You Have Always Wanted.* Easton: Harmony, 2010.

Amen, Daniel G. *Healing the Hardware of the Soul: How Making the Brain-Soul Connection Can Optimize Your Life, Love, and Spiritual Growth.* New York: Free Press, 2002.

Amen, Daniel G. *Images of Human Behavior: A Brain SPECT Atlas.* Newport Beach: Mindworks Press, 2004.

Amen, Daniel G. *Magnificent Mind at Any Age: Natural Ways to Unleash Your Brain's Maximum Potential.* New York: Three Rivers Press, 2009.

"Amygdala." ScienceDaily. Accessed January 24, 2017. https://www.sciencedaily.com/terms/amygdala.htm.

Bradberry, Travis, and Jean Greaves. *The Emotional Intelligence Quick Book.* New York: Fireside, 2005.

Colvin, Geoffrey. "Catch a Rising Star." *Fortune*, January 30, 2006.

Drucker, Peter F. *Managing in a Time of Great Change.* New York: Butterworth-Heinemann, 1995.

"Edward Thorndike" *Wikipedia*, last modified February 20, 2019, https://en.wikipedia.org/wiki/Edward_Thorndike#cite_note-14.

Erlandson, Eddie, and Kate Ludeman. "Coaching the Alpha Male." *Harvard Business Review,* May 2004.

Fields, R. Douglas. "Humans Are Genetically Predisposed to Kill Each Other." *Psychology Today* (blog), October 2, 2016. https://www.psychologytoday.com/us/blog/the-new-brain/201610/humans-are-genetically-predisposed-kill-each-other.

Ganim, Sara. "Exclusive: Jerry Sandusky Interview Prompts Long-Ago Victims to Contact Lawyer." *The Patriot News,* November 17, 2011. http://www.pennlive.com/midstate/index.ssf/2011/11/exclusive_jerry_sandusky_inter.html.

Gladwell, Malcolm. *Blink: The Power of Thinking Without Thinking.* New York: Little, Brown and Company, 2005.

Gladwell, Malcolm. *Outliers: The Story of Success.* New York: Little, Brown and Company, 2008.

Goleman, Daniel. *Emotional Intelligence: Why It Can Matter More Than IQ.* New York: Bantam, 1995.

Goleman, Daniel. *Social Intelligence: The New Science of Human Relationships.* New York: Bantam, 2006.

Goleman, Daniel. "What Makes a Leader?" *Harvard Business Review,* January 2004.

Goleman, Daniel. *Working with Emotional Intelligence.* New York: Bantam, 1998.

Goodwin, Doris Kearns. *Team of Rivals: The Political Genius of Abraham Lincoln.* New York: Simon & Schuster, 2005.

Hamilton, Ryan. *How You Decide: The Science of Human Decision Making.* DVD. Chantilly: The Teaching Company, 2016.

Hatesohl, Delmar, and Dick Lee. "Listening: Our Most Used Communications Skill." Last modified October 1993. https://extension2.missouri.edu/cm150.

"History of IQ Test." 123test. Accessed January 25, 2017. https://www.123test.com/history-of-IQ-test/.

Kanazawa, Satoshi. "Why Human Evolution Pretty Much Stopped about 10,000 Years Ago." *Psychology Today* (blog), October 16, 2008. https://www.psychologytoday.com/blog/the-scientific-fundamentalist/200810/why-human-evolution-pretty-much-stopped-about-10000-years.

Ledoux, Joseph. *Synaptic Self: How Our Brains Become Who We Are*. New York: Penguin Books, 2003.

Ledoux, Joseph. *The Emotional Brain: The Mysterious Underpinnings of Emotional Life*. New York: Simon and Schuster, 2015.

The Associated Press. "Penn State Settlements Covered 1971 Sandusky Abuse Claim." *USA Today*, May 9, 2016. https://www.usatoday.com/story/sports/ncaaf/2016/05/08/penn-state-settlements-jerry-sandusky-joe-paterno/84125254/.

Index

Symbols

60 *Minutes* 33

A

abstract intelligence 50
accountability 163, 170–72
    avoidance of 163–65
    game playing and 163–65
    goals and 173
active listening
    vs empathic listening 138–39
    key steps to 135–37
adrenaline 33, 105, 128, 157
    amygdala and 33
    empathetic listening and 139–41
adrenal medulla 33
adult learning theory 50
alcohol, as a truth serum 37
Alighieri, Dante 102
Alka Seltzer 43
alpha males 52, 56–57
Amazon 71
Amen Clinics 35, 36
Amen, Daniel 29, 45
American Idol 121
Americans With Disabilities Act 173, 183
amygdala 27–28
    adrenaline and 33
    branding and 44
    emotional brain and 42
    emotions and 27
    fight-or-flight response and 122
    left frontal lobe and 30
    nonverbal cues and 110–11
    nonverbal reactions and 27
    priming and 44
    social skills and 27
    thalamus physical proximity to 42
The Andy Griffith Show 8, 102
angel bullies 102. *See also* bullies
angel trolls 102. *See also* bullies
anger, proper use of 3–4
ANTS (automatic negative thoughts) 73
Aristotle 3
Armed Services Vocational Aptitude Battery (ASVAB) 51.
    See also Emotional Quotient (EQ) Assessment

assaults
    conflict and 182
    in the workplace 105, 123
assertiveness 70, 74–82
assessment vs treatment 183
Asshole: How I Got Rich & Happy by Not Giving a Damn About Anyone & How You Can, Too. 62
assholes 61–62, 74. *See also* emotional children
Assholes 62
Assholes: A Theory 61
Associated Press 116
ASVAB (Armed Services Vocational Aptitude Battery) 51
attackers 8, 100, 121–25, 171
    bomb throwing from 157
    communication and 121–25
    fight-or-flight response to 122–23
Audible 71
automatic emotional reactions. *See* emotional responses
automatic negative thoughts (ANTS) 73

B

Binet, Alfred 50
blind rage 37
Blink: The Power of Thinking Without Thinking 18, 19
blurting 129
bomb throwing
    consequences of 157–58
    fight-or-flight response and 157
bootlickers 157
Bradberry, Travis 10, 57–58
Brain and Creativity Institute at the University of Southern California 47
brains
    anatomy of 26
    chemicals in 40
    control of 25
    emotional vs logical 39, 148
    emotion, amygdala and 42
    frontal lobes and 28–38
    function of amygdala 27–28
    function of the thalamus 26
    health of and behavior 180
    neural junction box of 26

brains (continued)
   sleep and 29
   SPECT scans of 35
   spindle cells in 39
branding 43
   amygdala and 44
Brando, Marlon 54
Building a Civilized Workplace and Surviving One That
      Isn't 62
bullies 33, 116, 117, 171
   angel bullies 102
   angel trolls 102
   devil trolls 121
   retreaters enabling 116–17
Burger King 43
Burkin, Alice 19
Butch Cassidy and the Sundance Kid 7

C

caring vs managing 117
Change Your Brain, Change Your Life 45
children. *See* emotional children
Coaching the Alpha Male 52, 56–57
Columbia University 50
Colvin, Geoffrey 17
common ground 187
communication 95, 98
   attackers and 121–25
   being nice, re-examination of 115
   conversations 99
   disagreements and 115
   empathy and 138
   fight-or-flight response and 123
   good communicators. *See* honest and respectful
      communicators
   high stakes poker situations 113
   honest and respectful style of 125–29
   interpersonal 99–00
   nonverbal cues and 110–11
   poor communicators. *See* attackers; retreaters
   preparation 99–00
   self-control and 126
competence 51
complaints vs criticism 107
compliments vs rewards 161
computed tomography (CT) 35
conflict 9, 57. *See also* conflict resolution; emotional
      intelligence, conflict and
   assault and 182
   blurting and 129
   disagreements and 115
   exploding and 129
   initiating resolution of 133–34
   initial reactions to 45

trust and 9, 57
   understanding another's point of view and 147
   verbal 161
conflict resolution 93–94
   case study of 163–82
   choices for 101
   initiating 133–34
   passive-aggressive style 101
   retreaters and 101
   strategies for 161
   through Verbal Jeet 124
contempt 107–8
conversations 99. *See also* communication
   timing of 30
Corleone, Don Vito 53–54
Corleone, Michael 54
Corleone, Sonny 54, 57
cortisol 29, 122, 128, 140, 157
Covey, Stephen 71, 132
Cowell, Simon 8, 52, 74, 121, 149
Criminal Minds 160
critical decision-making. *See* decision-making
criticism vs complaints 107
customer service 171
   description of 4
   employee relations and 4–6
   listening and 133
   programs 64

D

Dalai Lama 1, 7
Damasio, Antonio 47
Darwinism 22
Dear Asshole 62
decision-making 46, 143
   emotional intelligence and 60
   emotions involvement in 46
   empathetic listening and 143
   new information and 156
defensiveness 108–9
deflection 164
Democratic National Committee 154
devil trolls 121. *See also* bullies
dialogue 99. *See also* communication
DiCaprio, Leonardo 24
direct evidence 184
disagreement 154–56
   communication and 115
   conflict and 115
   handling of 115
   between intelligent people 154
   opinions causing 154–58
   rewards and 159
   throwing bombs and 157

understanding and 155
value systems and 155
discrimination 139
Disney World 43
diversion 164, 177
divorce 113
disagreements and 115
dopamine 40
Dr. Phil 163
Drucker, Peter 67
Dumbledore, Albus 53

E

ego 148
opinions and 155
Einstein, Albert 12
Elliott, Jane 138
emotional children 7, 10, 17, 52, 55, 58–62, 66–67,
89, 103, 117, 123, 150
emotional expression 70, 82–83
emotional hijacking 3, 4, 45, 95, 122, 141, 182
amygdala and 31
blind rage and 37
emotional intelligence (EI) 5, 9, 13, 92, 166. *See
also* emotional intelligence skills
alpha males and 52, 56–57
assessment 117
Big Five factors of 68–73
communication and 53, 59, 66–67, 126
conflict and 61, 81, 92
decision-making and 60
disagreement and 155
emotional control and 59, 80
empathic listening and 141
empathy and 60, 138
essence of 166
flexibility of 51
future success and 51, 57, 65
high performers and 10, 65
importance of 10
impulse control and 25
increase of 51–52, 80–81
leadership and 11, 66
management and 58, 65
personal achievement and 11, 51
programs and 62–64, 66–67
role models for 54
self-help strategies for 68–73
sleep and 29–30
strategies 183
talking to yourself and 46
team building and 7, 10
vs technical competence 16, 65, 78
trust and 60, 80

The Emotional Intelligence Quick Book 10
emotional intelligence skills
decision-making 68, 71–72
interpersonal 68, 70–71
self-expression 68, 70–71
self-perception 68–69
stress management 68, 72–73, 86–89
Emotional Quotient (EQ) Assessment 46, 84, 86,
178, 183
Big Five 68
categories 51
EQ-i 2.0 assessment 68
interviews and 84–86
results 57, 73–89
Emotional Quotient Inventory test 68
emotional responses
automatic 23
fight-or-flight 23
outbursts 182
emotional self-awareness 69
emotional systems 3, 10, 68, 95
fight-or-flight response and 38
inaccuracy of 45
emotions
amygdala and 27
brain's thermostat for 30
control of 54–55, 57–59, 68, 92
leadership and 17
vs logic 3, 22, 56
neurology of 22–26
speed of 24, 39
empathic listening 5, 134, 167–69, 175. *See
also* empathic listening, parroting, and
"rewards" (EPR)
vs active listening 138–39
adrenaline and 139–41
as a critical skill 139–42
decision-making and 143
emotional intelligence and 141
honest and respectful communicators and 139
information gathering during 142
parroting and 147–48
point of view of others and 146–47
respect and 141
rewards during 140
understanding and 148
empathic listening, parroting, and "rewards" (EPR) 5,
8, 65, 92, 94–95, 116, 183
empathy 70, 74–82, 82–83, 86–89, 133, 138, 160
communication and 138
emotional intelligence and 138
interpersonal relationships and 147
physicians and 19
training 138

Employee Assistance Program (EAP) 179, 183
employee relations 171
    customer service and 4–6, 83
    description of 4
    programs 63
employees
    cost of 5
    treatment of 5
enablers 116–21
    rules of 103
endangerment 38, 158
epinephrine 33
EPR (empathic listening, parroting, and "rewards").
    See empathic listening, parroting, and
    "rewards" (EPR)
Erlandson, Eddie 52, 56
Ethical Culture Fieldston School 13
evidence, direct 184
evolution of humans 22
excellence, standard of 11
exploding and conflict 129
eye contact 168

F

Family and Medical Leave Act (FMLA) 116
FedEx 5
feelings. *See also* emotions
    conflict resolution and 149
    parroting and 149
Fields, R. Douglas 25
fight-or-flight response 23, 59, 100, 102, 105, 166
    amygdala and 122
    attackers creating 122–23
    blood flow during 34
    bomb throwing and 157
    communication and 123
    details of 32–34
    emotional systems and 38
    temporary autism and 34
flexibility 72
Flintstone, Fred 22, 23, 25, 32, 42, 45
FMLA (Family and Medical Leave Act) 116
Fonda, Henry 155
Forman, Red 1, 7, 55
Fortune 15, 17, 193
four horsemen of the apocalypse 106–15
    contempt 107–8
    criticism 107
    defensiveness 108
    honesty and 129
    stonewalling 109
French Ministry of Education 50
frontal lobes 28–38
    blood flow to 29

    brain scans of 35
    control of emotions and 30
    left, amygdala and 30
    timing of conversations and 30
Fulghum, Robert 154

G

games
    accountability and 163–65
    deflection 164
    diversion 164, 177
    stonewalling 165
    victim mentality 165, 177
Ganim, Sara 116
General Custer 156
General Motors 18
Gibson, Mel 37
Gladwell, Malcolm 11, 18
Glass Bottle Blowers union 150
goals and accountability 173
Godfather 53–54
Goizueta Business School at Emory University 29
Goleman, Daniel 10, 17
Goodwin, Doris Kearns 53
gossip 110, 184–87
    grapevine and 184
    retreaters and 105–6
    trust and 111
go-to people 15, 15–19
    identification of 15
    promotion of 17
    trust and 16
The Gottman Institute 106–15
Gottman, John 106, 108, 114, 129
grapevines and gossip 184
The Great Courses 72
Greaves, Jean 10, 57–58
groupthink 157
Gump, Forrest 74

H

hair-trigger reactions 25
Hall, Marcus 54
Hamilton, Ryan 29
Harris v. Forklift Systems 171
Harry Potter 53
Harvard Business Review 17, 52
Harvard Law Review 155
Harvard Law School 155
Hay/McBer 10
health and honesty 128–29
hearing vs listening 134
hearsay 184
heart attacks 33

high performers and emotional intelligence 10
High Road 45
high stakes poker situations 113–15, 126–27
hijacking. *See* emotional hijacking
honest and respectful communicators 100
    empathic listening and 139
    empathy and 139
honesty
    attackers and 121
    benefits of 128–30
    four horsemen of the apocalypse and 129
    health and 128–29
    judgment and 128
    retreaters and 110
humans
    evolution of 22
    homicidal nature of 25
    as prey 22
hypersensitivity vs offensive, test for 171

I

improvement plans 180
impulse control 71
    emotional intelligence and 25
independence 70, 74–82
Inferno 102, 121
intellectual development
    goals and 50
    main areas of 50
intelligence. *See also* emotional intelligence (EI)
    abstract 50
    mechanical 50
    social 50–51
intelligence quotient (IQ) 50–58
Intelligence Quotient test (IQ test) 50, 68
    shortcomings of 50
interpersonal
    communication 99–00
interpersonal relationships 70, 74–78, 82–83, 86–89
    empathy and 147

J

James, Aaron 61
Jeet Kune Do 93
judgment 128
Jun Fan Gung Fu Institute 92
jungle environments 111, 158

K

Kanazawa, Satoshi 22
kill strikes 6, 8, 131, 145, 153

L

Langan, Christopher 11–13

Laugh Factory 37
leadership
    alpha males and 56–57
    emotional intelligence and 11
    emotions and 17
    programs 63
    rules of 102–3
LeDoux, Joseph 42
Lee, Bruce 92–93
Levinson, Wendy 18
limbic system 27
Lincoln, Abraham 53
listening 132–44. *See also* empathic listening; *See also* active listening
    customer service and 133
    how to 134–35
    respect and 132
logic 182
    vs emotions 3, 68
Low Road 45
Ludeman, Kate 52, 56

M

magic bullet 173, 175, 179, 181, 184, 186
magnetic resonance imaging (MRI) 35
Magnificent Mind at Any Age: Natural Ways to Unleash Your Brain's Maximum Potential 29
malicious obedience 165
malpractice
    lawyer 19
    physicians and 18
    reason for 18
managers
    caring and 117
    motivation and 18
Managing in a Time of Great Change 67
Man, Wong Jack 92
martial arts 92–93
martyrs. *See* victim mentality
McCain, John 154
McDonalds 43
McKinley Irvin 112
McQueary, Mike 116
mechanical intelligence 50
MetLife 65
Military Entrance Processing Stations (MEPS) 51
military, prediction of success in 50–51
mind blind 174
Mirage Hotel 27
mirror neurons 167
Montana State University 12
Multi-Health Systems Inc. (MHS) 68, 74

N

Neff, Tom 17
nervous system, parasympathetic 33
neural junction box 26, 39, 41
neurology 160
neurons
    mirror 167
neurons, spindle cell 39
nice, re-examination of 115
Nicomachean Ethics 3
Nike 43
The No Asshole Rule 62
nonverbal cues 110–11, 174
nonverbal reactions
    amygdala and 27
    sending positive 167

O

Obama, Barack 154
Occupational Safety and Health Administration
        (OSHA) 31, 53
offensive vs hypersensitivity, test for 171
Ohio State University 46, 54, 94, 130
opinions
    disagreement and 154–58
    ego and 155
    married to 155–58
    vs personal value 158–59
    rewards and 159
    validation and 161
Oppenheimer, Robert 11
    childhood of 13–14
optimism 72, 82–83
organizational communication 14. *See
        also* communication
OSHA (Occupational Safety and Health
        Administration) 31, 53
Outliers: The Story of Success 11
outplacement firms 18
Owens Corning Fiberglass 150

P

parasympathetic nervous system 33
parroting 146, 160, 169, 176, 181
    empathic listening and 147–48
    feelings and 148
    understanding and 146–48
passive-aggressive 8, 57, 59, 62, 101–6, 108, 110, 126,
        129, 169
    style of conflict resolution 101
Paterno, Joe 116
The Patriot News 116
Payne, Keith 34
Penn State University 116

personal achievement and emotional intelligence 11
personal competence 51
personal value vs personal opinion 158–59
persuasion 13
physicians
    empathy and 19
    malpractice and 18
piloerection 23
point of view 159
priming 44
problem-recognition stage (of Verbal Jeet) 167–72,
        178
problem-solving 71, 86–89
problem-solving stage (of Verbal Jeet) 172–73, 178
programs 62–64
    change management 63
    customer service 64
    emotional intelligence and 66
    employee relations 63
    leadership 63
    production and quality 64
    safety 63
    sales 64
    teambuilding 63
    workplace violence 64
promotion of go-to people 17
Psychology Today 22, 25

R

rapid eye movement (REM) 29
reactions, hair-trigger 25
reality testing 71, 86–89
receivers 99–00
    listening and 135–37
Reed College 12
relationships. *See* employee relations; interpersonal
        relationships
    contempt in 107–8
    criticism in 107
    defensiveness in 108
    stonewalling in 109
REM (rapid eye movement) 29
Republican National Committee 154
respect 141, 148
    empathetic listening and 141
    listening and 132
    validation and 161
retreaters 8, 100–121, 170, 185
    bullying and 116
    communication from 106
    conflict resolution and 101
    dishonesty and 110
    divorce and 113
    as enablers 116–21

enabling bullies 116–17
gossip and 105–6
jungle environments created by 111
as Machiavellians 110
response to attackers 158
rubber band effect and 109
tactics for dealing with 103–4
trust and 106
The Revenant 24
rewards 156, 168, 176–77, 181, 186. *See also* validation
vs agreement with 159
vs compliments 161
disagreement and 159, 169
during empathic listening 140
opinions and 159
understanding and 162
Richards, Michael 37
Right Management Consultants 18
Rose, Pete 7
rubber band effect 109
rules of enablers 103
rules of leadership 102–3

S

Sandusky, Jerry 116
savvy. *See* emotional intelligence (EI)
Seinfeld 37
self-
actualization 69
awareness, emotional 69
control and communication 126
esteem 157, 161
regard 69
senders 95, 98, 99–00, 121, 123, 125, 126, 135–38, 158
serotonin 40
Simon-Binet IQ test 50
Simon, Théodore 50
single photon emission computerized tomography (SPECT) blood-flow scans 35
skills. *See also* interpersonal skills
soft 94
sleep
cortisol and 29
Rapid Eye Movement (REM) and 29
social
competence 51
intelligence 50–51
responsibility 70, 82–83
skills and the amygdala 27
soft skills 94
solutions 187
sounding boards 127

SPECT (single photon emission computerized tomography) blood-flow scans 35
Spencer Stewart (headhunters for) 17
spindle cell neurons 39
Sports Illustrated 54
stabbing in the back. *See* gossip; honesty; retreaters; trust
standard of excellence 11
Star Wars 53
Stewart, Jimmy 155
stonewalling 109, 165
rubber band effect and 109
stress
conflict and 57
temporary autism and 34
tolerance 72, 78–82
stupidity 154
subconscious mind and influencing behavior 43
systems
emotional 3
limbic 27

T

talking to yourself, value of 46
Team of Rivals: The Political Genius of Abraham Lincoln 53
technical competence vs savvy 16
temporarily autistic 34
testing. *See also* Armed Services Vocational Aptitude Battery (ASVAB); *See also* Emotional Quotient (EQ) Assessment; *See also* Intelligence Quotient test (IQ test)
reality 71, 86–89
thalamus 26
amygdala physical proximity to 42
That '70s Show 1
theories
of adult learning 50
of civil disobedience 53
Thoreau, Henry David 53
Thorndike, Edward 50
thought, speed of 38–46
three-year-old syndrome 109
throwing bombs
disagreement and 157
trust and 157
treatment vs assessment 183
trolls. *See* bullies
trust 187
conflict and 57
definition of 8
disagreement and 9
earning 9
emotional intelligence and 60, 80

trust (continued)
  gossip and 111
  throwing bombs and 157

U

understanding
  disagreement and 155
  ego and 148
  rewards and 162
United Steelworkers 150
University of Cambridge 13
University of Chicago 12
University of Maryland, College Park 25
University of North Carolina at Chapel Hill 34
University of Southern California 47
University of Washington 114
USA Today 171, 177, 178, 182
U.S. Department of Defense 51

V

validation. *See also* rewards
  vs agreement 161
  respect and 161
values and disagreement 155
vasopressin 40
Verbal Jeet 4, 5, 6, 92, 94, 163, 181. *See also* Verbal
      Jeet Skills

black belt 8, 95
coaching process 167–78
conflict resolution and 124
kill strikes 8, 92–95
as life skills 181
problem-recognition stage 167–72, 174–78
problem-solving stage 172–73, 178–80
stance 166–67, 175, 185
Verbal Jeet Skills 9, 65, 70–71, 81, 107, 116, 147, 156,
      163, 171, 185, 187
  gossip and 185
victim mentality 165, 177
  malicious obedience and 165

W

Wayne, John 52, 147
workplaces
  assaults in 105, 123
  dangers in 31, 53
  violence programs 64
World War I 50

Y

Yale University 11
Yoda 53

About the Author

Scott Warrick has been working as a human resource (HR) professional and employment and labor attorney for almost 40 years. Throughout the last four decades, he has practiced as a traditional employment and labor attorney, an in-house HR professional, and as an HR consultant. In 2001, Scott started his own HR consulting, coaching, and training practice alongside his employment and labor law practice. He uses his dual background in HR and employment law to prevent legal issues while simultaneously improving employee relations. His goal is very clear:

"To solve employee problems before *they happen."*

Scott believes that all lawsuits and acts of workplace violence can be prevented if humans learn emotional intelligence in order to overcome their basic caveman instincts and resolve conflicts rather than suppressing and escalating them. The ultimate comedian/trainer, he has worked with hundreds of organizations to put proper human resource measures in place, as well as coaching and training managers and employees in over 50 different topics in his own unique, practical, entertaining, and humorous style. Scott now travels the country presenting his various programs to private and public sector organizations alike. He is also a six-time presenter at SHRM's National Diversity Conferences, presenting his unique and humorous lecture, "Tolerance and Diversity for White Guys...And Other Human Beings."

Scott's "Do It Yourself HR Department & Legal Compliance" program is a favorite among human resource professionals across the country to not only inform clients of the changes in Employment Law, but to also bring their departments into compliance—and keep them there! He has also literally "written the book" on employment and labor law; *The HR Professional's Guide To Employment and Labor Law* is now over 1,600 pages and used at several colleges and universities.

Scott has also received the Ohio State Human Resource Council's David Prize for Creativity in Human Resource Management in 1991, and the Human Resource Association of Central Ohio's Linda Kerns Award for Outstanding Creativity in the Field of Human Resource Management in 2000. In 2007, Scott earned his Certified Emotional Quotient Counselor certificate from Dr. Rich Handley, one of the pioneers in this field and an associate of Dr. Reuven Bar-On, the creator of the BarOn EQ-i® test, the most widely used EQ test in the world. In 2008, *CEO Magazine* named Scott a "Human Resources Superstar." In 2009, Scott was the first civilian to be awarded the Nebraska Army National Guard's Believe and Succeed Medal for Achievement Beyond The Call Of Duty for his program which combined his emotional intelligence seminar and his conflict resolution program, Verbal Jeet (or "EPR"). In 2012, *Columbus Business First* named Scott as one of the "20 People in Human Resources To Know."

Scott holds his BA degree in organizational communication and his master's degree in labor and human resources from The Ohio State University. Scott also holds a law degree from Capital University College of Law (class valedictorian: 1st out of 233 students).

Other SHRM Titles

A Manager's Guide to Developing Competencies in HR Staff
Tips and Tools for Improving Proficiency in Your Reports
Phyllis G. Hartman, SHRM-SCP

Actualized Leadership
Meeting Your Shadow and Maximizing Your Potential
William L. Sparks

California Employment Law: A Guide for Employers
Revised and Updated 2018 Edition
James J. McDonald, Jr., JD

Digital HR
A Guide to Technology-Enabled HR
Deborah Waddill, Ed.D.

Extinguish Burnout
A Practical Guide to Prevention and Recovery
Robert Bogue and Terri Bogue

From Hello to Goodbye: Second Edition
Proactive Tips for Maintaining Positive Employee Relations
Christine V. Walters, JD, SHRM-SCP

From We Will to At Will
A Handbook for Veteran Hiring, Transitioning, and Thriving in the Workplace
Justin Constantine with Andrew Morton

Go Beyond the Job Description
A 100-Day Action Plan for Optimizing Talents and Building Engagement
Ashley Prisant Lesko, Ph.D., SHRM-SCP

The HR Career Guide
Great Answers to Tough Career Questions
Martin Yate, CPC

HR on Purpose!!
Developing Deliberate People Passion
Steve Browne, SHRM-SCP

Investing in People
Financial Impact of Human Resource Initiatives, 3rd edition
Wayne F. Cascio, John W. Boudreau, and Alexis A. Fink

Mastering Consultation as an HR Practitioner
Making an Impact on Small Businesses
Jennifer Currence, SHRM-SCP

Motivation-Based Interviewing
A Revolutionary Approach to Hiring the Best
Carol Quinn

The 9 Faces of HR
Discovering HR Disruptors that Add Value, Drive Change, and Champion Innovation
Kris Dunn

The Practical Guide to HR Analytics
Using Data to Inform, Transform, and Empower HR Decisions
Shonna D. Waters, Valerie N. Streets, Lindsay A. McFarlane, and Rachel Johnson-Murray

The Power of Stay Interviews for Engagement and Retention
Second Edition
Richard P. Finnegan

Predicting Business Success
Using Smarter Analytics to Drive Results
Scott Mondore, Hannah Spell, Matt Betts, and Shane Douthitt

The Recruiter's Handbook
A Complete Guide for Sourcing, Selecting, and Engaging the Best Talent
Sharlyn Lauby, SHRM-SCP

The SHRM Essential Guide to Employment Law
A Handbook for HR Professionals, Managers, and Businesses
Charles H. Fleischer, JD

The Talent Fix
A Leader's Guide to Recruiting Great Talent
Tim Sackett, SHRM-SCP

Books Approved for SHRM Recertification Credits

107 Frequently Asked Questions About Staffing Management, Fiester
(ISBN: 9781586443733)

47 Frequently Asked Questions About the Family and Medical Leave Act, Fiester
(ISBN: 9781586443801)

57 Frequently Asked Questions About Workplace Safety and Security, Fiester
(ISBN: 9781586443610)

97 Frequently Asked Questions About Compensation, Fiester
(ISBN: 9781586443566)

A Manager's Guide to Developing Competencies in HR Staff, Hartman
(ISBN: 9781586444365)

A Necessary Evil: Managing Employee Activity on Facebook, Wright
(ISBN: 9781586443412)

Aligning Human Resources and Business Strategy, Holbeche
(ISBN: 9780750680172)

Applying Critical Evaluation: Making an Impact in Small Business, Currence
(ISBN: 9781586444426)

Becoming the Evidence Based Manager, Latham
(ISBN: 9780891063988)

Being Global: How to Think, Act, and Lead in a Transformed World, Cabrera
(ISBN: 9781422183229)

Black Holes and White Spaces: Reimagining the Future of Work and HR, Boudreau
(ISBN: 9781586444617)

Business Literacy Survival Guide for HR Professionals, Garey
(ISBN: 9781586442057)

Business-Focused HR: 11 Processes to Drive Results, Mondore
(ISBN: 9781586442040)

Calculating Success, Hoffman
(ISBN: 9781422166390)

California Employment Law, Revised and Updated, McDonald
(ISBN: 9781586444815)

Collaborate: The Art of We, Sanker
(ISBN: 9781118114728)

Deep Dive: Proven Method for Building Strategy, Horwath
(ISBN: 9781929774821)

Defining HR Success: 9 Critical Competencies for HR Professionals, Alonso
(ISBN: 9781586443825)

Destination Innovation: HR's Role in Charting the Course, Buhler
(ISBN: 9781586443832)

Developing Business Acumen, Currence
(ISBN: 9781586444143)

*Developing Proficiency in HR: 7 Self-Directed
Activities for HR Professionals*, Cohen
(ISBN: 9781586444167)

*Digital HR: A Guide to Technology- Enabled
Human Resources*, Waddill
(ISBN: 9781586445423)

*Diverse Teams at Work: Capitalizing on the Power of
Diversity*, Gardenswartz
(ISBN: 9781586440367)

*Effective Human Resource Management: A Global
Analysis*, Lawler
(ISBN: 9780804776875)

Emotional Intelligence 2.0, Bradberry
(ISBN: 9780974320625)

Financial Analysis for HR Managers, Director
(ISBN: 9780133925425)

From Hello to Goodbye, 2e, Walters
(ISBN: 9781586444471)

*From We Will to at Will: A Handbook for Veteran
Hiring*, Constantine
(ISBN: 9781586445072)

Give Your Company a Fighting Chance, Danaher
(ISBN: 9781586443658)

Go Beyond the Job Description, Lesko
(ISBN: 9781586445171)

*Good People, Bad Managers: How Work Culture
Corrupts Good Intentions*, Culbert
(ISBN: 9780190652395)

*Got a Minute? The 9 Lessons Every HR Professional
Must Learn to Be Successful*, Dwyer
(ISBN: 9781586441982)

*Got a Solution? HR Approaches to 5 Common and
Persistent Business Problems*, Dwyer
(ISBN: 9781586443665)

*Handbook for Strategic HR: Best Practices in
Organization Development*, Vogelsang
(ISBN: 9780814432495)

*Hidden Drivers of Success: Leveraging Employee
Insights for Strategic Advantage*, Schiemann
(ISBN: 9781586443337)

*HR at Your Service: Lessons from Benchmark Service
Organizations*, Latham
(ISBN: 9781586442477)

*HR on Purpose: Developing Deliberate People
Passion*, Browne
(ISBN: 9781586444259)

*HR Transformation: Building Human Resources from
the Inside Out*, Ulrich
(ISBN: 9780071638708)

*HR's Greatest Challenge: Driving the C-Suite to
Improve Employee Engagement ...*, Finnegan
(ISBN: 9781586443795)

*Humanity Works: Merging Technologies and People
for the Workforce of the Future*, Levit
(ISBN: 9780749483456)

*Investing in People: Financial Impact of Human
Resource Initiatives*, 2e, Boudreau
(ISBN: 9780132394116)

*Investing in What Matters: Linking Employees to
Business Outcomes*, Mondore
(ISBN: 9781586441371)

*Leadership from the Mission Control Room to the
Boardroom*, Hill
(ISBN: 9780998634319)

Leading an HR Transformation, Anderson
(ISBN: 9781586444860)

Leading the Unleadable, Willett
(ISBN: 9780814437605)

Leading with Dignity, Hicks
(ISBN: 9780300229639)

Lean HR: Introducing Process Excellence to Your Practice, Lay
(ISBN: 9781481914208)

Linkage Inc.'s Best Practices for Succession Planning: Case Studies, Research, Models, Tools, Sobol
(ISBN: 9780787985790)

Looking to Hire an HR Leader, Hartman
(ISBN: 9781586443672)

Manager 3.0: A Millennial's Guide to Rewriting the Rules of Management, Karsh
(ISBN: 9780814432891)

Manager Onboarding: 5 Steps for Setting New Leaders Up for Success, Lauby
(ISBN: 9781586444075)

Manager's Guide to Employee Engagement, Carbonara
(ISBN: 9780071799508)

Managing Employee Turnover, Allen
(ISBN: 9781606493403)

Managing the Global Workforce, Caligiuri
(ISBN: 9781405107327)

Managing the Mobile Workforce: Leading, Building, and Sustaining Virtual Teams, Clemons
(ISBN: 9780071742207)

Managing the Older Worker: How to Prepare for the New Organizational Order, Cappelli
(ISBN: 9781422131657)

Mastering Consultation as an HR Practitioner, Currence
(ISBN: 9781586445027)

Measuring ROI in Employee Relations and Compliance, Phillips
(ISBN: 9781586443597)

Motivation-Based Interviewing: A Revolutionary Approach to Hiring the Best, Quinn
(ISBN: 9781586445478)

Multipliers: How the Best Leaders Make Everyone Smarter, Wiseman
(ISBN: 9780061964398)

Negotiation at Work: Maximize Your Team's Skills with 60 High-Impact Activities, Asherman
(ISBN: 9780814431900)

New Power: How Power Works in Our Hyperconnected World, Heimans
(ISBN: 9780385541114)

Nine Minutes on Monday: The Quick and Easy Way to Go from Manager to Leader, Robbins
(ISBN: 9780071801980)

One Life: How Organisations Can Leverage Work-Life Integration, Uhereczky
(ISBN: 9782874035180)

One Strategy: Organizing, Planning and Decision Making, Sinofsky
(ISBN: 9780470560457)

Organizational Design that Sticks, Albrecht
(ISBN: 9781948699006)

Peer Coaching at Work, Parker
(ISBN: 9780804797092)

People Analytics: How Social Sensing Technology Will Transform Business, Waber
(ISBN: 9780133158311)

Perils and Pitfalls of California Employment Law: A Guide for HR Professionals, Effland
(ISBN: 9781586443634)

Point Counterpoint II: New Perspectives on People & Strategy, Vosburgh
(ISBN: 9781586444181)

Point Counterpoint: New Perspectives on People & Strategy, Tavis
(ISBN: 9781586442767)

Practices for Engaging the 21st-Century Workforce, Castellano
(ISBN: 9780133086379)

Predicting Business Success: Using Smarter Analytics to Drive Results, Mondore
(ISBN: 9781586445379)

Preventing Workplace Harassment in a #MeToo World, Dominick
(ISBN: 9781586445539)

Proving the Value of HR: How and Why to Measure ROI, Phillips
(ISBN: 9781586442316)

Reality Based Leadership, Wakeman
(ISBN: 9780470613504)

Reinventing Jobs: A 4-Step Approach for Applying Automation to Work, Jesuthasan
(ISBN: 9781633694071)

Rethinking Retention in Good Times and Bad, Finnegan
(ISBN: 9780891062387)

Social Media Strategies for Professionals and Their Firms, Golden
(ISBN: 9780470633106)

Solving the Compensation Puzzle: Putting Together a Complete Pay and Performance System, Koss
(ISBN: 9781586440923)

StandOut 2.0: Assess Your Strengths, Find Your Edge, Win at Work, Buckingham
(ISBN: 9781633690745)

Stop Bullying at Work, 2e, Daniel
(ISBN: 9781586443856)

Talent, Transformation, and the Triple Bottom Line, Savitz
(ISBN: 9781118140970)

The ACE Advantage: How Smart Companies Unleash Talent for Optimal Performance, Schiemann
(ISBN: 9781586442866)

The Big Book of HR, Mitchell
(ISBN: 9781601631893)

The Circle Blueprint: Decoding the Conscious and Unconscious Factors …, Skeen
(ISBN: 9781119434856)

The Crowdsourced Performance Review, Mosley
(ISBN: 9780071817981)

The Cultural Fit Factor: Creating an Employment Brand That Attracts …, Pellet
(ISBN: 9781586441265)

The Definitive Guide to HR Communication, Davis
(ISBN: 9780137061433)

The Employee Engagement Mindset, Clark
(ISBN: 9780071788298)

The EQ Interview: Finding Employees with High Emotional Intelligence, Lynn
(ISBN: 9780814409411)

The Global Challenge: International Human Resource Management, 2nd ed., Evans
(ISBN: 9780073530376)

The Global M&A Tango, Trompenaars
(ISBN: 9780071761154)

The Hard Talk Handbook: The Definitive Guide to Having the Difficult Conversations …, Metcalfe (ASIN: B07J2C8YF5)

The HR Answer Book, 2e, Smith
(ISBN: 9780814417171)

The HR Career Guide: Great Answers to Tough Career Questions, Yate
(ISBN: 9781586444761)

The HR Insider: How to Land Your Dream Job, and Keep It!, Jeshani
(ISBN: 9781717475565)

The Manager's Guide to HR, 2e, Muller
(ISBN: 9780814433027)

The Performance Appraisal Tool Kit, Falcone
(ISBN: 9780814432631)

The Power of Appreciative Inquiry: A Practical Guide to Positive Change, 2nd ed., Whitney
(ISBN: 9781605093284)

The Power of Stay Interviews for Retention and Engagement, 2e, Finnegan
(ISBN: 9781586445126)

The Practical Guide to HR Analytics, Waters
(ISBN: 9781586445324)

The Recruiter's Handbook, Lauby
(ISBN: 9781586444655)

The SHRM Essential Guide to Employment Law, Fleischer
(ISBN: 9781586444709)

The Square and the Triangle: The Power of Integrating Relationships …, Stevens
(ISBN: 9781612061474)

The Talent Fix: A Leader's Guide to Recruiting Great Talent, Sackett
(ISBN: 9781586445225)

Thinking in Bets: Making Smarter Decisions When You Don't Have All the Facts, Duke
(ISBN: 9780735216358)

Thrive By Design: The Neuroscience That Drives High-Performance Cultures, Rheem
(ISBN: 9781946633064)

Touching People's Lives: Leaders' Sorrow or Joy, Losey
(ISBN: 9781586444310)

Transformational Diversity, Citkin
(ISBN: 9781586442309)

Transformative HR: How Great Companies Use Evidence-Based Change …, Boudreau
(ISBN: 9781118036044)

Type R: Transformative Resilience for Thriving in a Turbulent World, Marston
(ISBN: 9781610398060)

Up, Down, and Sideways: High-Impact Verbal Communication for HR Professionals, Buhler
(ISBN: 9781586443375)

View from the Top: Leveraging Human and Organization Capital to Create Value, Wright
(ISBN: 9781586444006)

WE: Men, Women, and the Decisive Formula for Winning at Work, Anderson
(ISBN: 9781119524694)

Weathering Storms: Human Resources in Difficult Times, SHRM
(ISBN: 9781586441340)

What If? Short Stories to Spark Diversity Dialogue, Robbins
(ISBN: 9780891062752)

What Is Global Leadership? 10 Key Behaviors that Define Great Global Leaders, Gundling
(ISBN: 9781904838234)

Winning the War for Talent in Emerging Markets: Why Women are the Solution, Hewlett
(ISBN: 9781422160602)

Work Rules!: Insights from Inside Google That Will Transform How You Live and Lead, Bock
(ISBN: 9781455554799)